CliffsNotes™
Getting Started in Online Investing

By Jill Gilbert

IN THIS BOOK

- Decide whether online investing is for you
- Research stocks, bonds, and mutual funds online
- Open your online account and make your first online trade
- Track your portfolio
- Reinforce what you learn with CliffsNotes Review
- Find more online investing information in CliffsNotes Resource Center and online at www.cliffsnotes.com

IDG Books Worldwide, Inc.
An International Data Group Company
Foster City, CA • Chicago, IL • Indianapolis, IN • New York, NY

About the Author

Jill Gilbert is a Certified Public Accountant and attorney. She has authored several books for IDG Books Worldwide, Inc., including *CliffsNotes Balancing Your Checkbook with Quicken* and *pcAnywhere For Dummies*.

Publisher's Acknowledgments

Editorial

Senior Project Editor: Kyle Looper
Acquisitions Editor: Laura Moss
Copy Editor: Stephanie Koutek
Technical Editor: Gene Bednarek

Production

Indexer: York Production Services
Proofreader: York Production Services
IDG Books Indianapolis Production Department

CliffsNotes™ Getting Started in Online Investing

Published by
IDG Books Worldwide, Inc.
An International Data Group Company
919 E. Hillsdale Blvd.
Suite 400
Foster City, CA 94404
www.idgbooks.com (IDG Books Worldwide Web site)
www.cliffsnotes.com (CliffsNotes Web site)

Library of Congress Catalog Card No.: 00-101153
ISBN: 0-7645-8540-1
Printed in the United States of America
10 9 8 7 6 5 4 3 2 1
1O/SW/QV/QQ/IN
Distributed in the United States by IDG Books Worldwide, Inc.
Distributed by CDG Books Canada Inc. for Canada; by Transworld Publishers Limited in the United Kingdom; by IDG Norge Books for Norway; by IDG Sweden Books for Sweden; by IDG Books Australia Publishing Corporation Pty. Ltd. for Australia and New Zealand; by TransQuest Publishers Pte Ltd. for Singapore, Malaysia, Thailand, Indonesia, and Hong Kong; by Gotop Information Inc. for Taiwan; by ICG Muse, Inc. for Japan; by Intersoft for South Africa; by Eyrolles for France; by International Thomson Publishing for Germany, Austria and Switzerland; by Distribuidora Cuspide for Argentina; by LR International for Brazil; by Galileo Libros for Chile; by Ediciones ZETA S.C.R. Ltda. for Peru; by WS Computer Publishing Corporation, Inc., for the Philippines; by Contemporanea de Ediciones for Venezuela; by Express Computer Distributors for the Caribbean and West Indies; by Micronesia Media Distributor, Inc. for Micronesia; by Chips Computadoras S.A. de C.V. for Mexico; by Editorial Norma de Panama S.A. for Panama; by American Bookshops for Finland.
For general information on IDG Books Worldwide's books in the U.S., please call our Consumer Customer Service department at 800-762-2974. For reseller information, including discounts and premium sales, please call our Reseller Customer Service department at 800-434-3422.
For information on where to purchase IDG Books Worldwide's books outside the U.S., please contact our International Sales department at 317-596-5530 or fax 317-572-4002.
For consumer information on foreign language translations, please contact our Customer Service department at 1-800-434-3422, fax 317-572-4002, or e-mail rights@idgbooks.com.
For information on licensing foreign or domestic rights, please phone +1-650-653-7098.
For sales inquiries and special prices for bulk quantities, please contact our Order Services department at 800-434-3422 or write to the address above.
For information on using IDG Books Worldwide's books in the classroom or for ordering examination copies, please contact our Educational Sales department at 800-434-2086 or fax 317-572-4005.
For press review copies, author interviews, or other publicity information, please contact our Public Relations department at 650-653-7000 or fax 650-653-7500.
For authorization to photocopy items for corporate, personal, or educational use, please contact Copyright Clearance Center, 222 Rosewood Drive, Danvers, MA 01923, or fax 978-750-4470.

Table of Contents

INTRODUCTION

Online investing takes you to the epicenter of financial markets all over the world with a click of your mouse. It also affords you instant access to the kind of sophisticated research and analysis you could formerly get only by paying substantial commissions to a full-service broker. Now you can execute your own trades at your convenience — even after the exchanges have closed for the day — at a big discount.

Why Do You Need This Book?

Can you answer yes to any of these questions?

- Do you need to learn about online investing fast?

- Don't have time to read 500 pages about online brokerages?

- Do you want to know about the best Web sites for gathering information about stocks, bonds, and mutual funds?

- Do you want to minimize brokerage commissions and transaction costs?

If so, then CliffsNotes *Getting Started in Online Investing* is for you!

How to Use This Book

You can read this book straight through or just look for the information you need. You can find information on a particular topic in a number of ways: You can search the index in the back of the book, locate your topic in the Table of Contents, or read the In This Chapter list in each chapter. To reinforce your learning, check out the Review and

Resource Center in the back of the book. To help you find important information in the book, look for the following icons in the text:

This icon reminds you of important information, practices, and investing concepts that you shouldn't forget in even the most volatile investment scenario.

This icon points out an investment practice or resource that can improve the profitability of your portfolio.

This icon alerts you to an investment trap or unsound practice that can cost you money.

Don't Miss Our Web Site

Keep up with the changing world of the Internet by visiting our Web site at www.cliffsnotes.com. Here's what you'll find:

- Interactive tools that are fun and informative
- Links to interesting Web sites
- Additional resources to help you continue your learning.

At www.cliffsnotes.com you can even register for a new feature called CliffsNotes Daily, which offers you newsletters on a variety of topics, delivered right to your e-mail inbox each business day.

If you haven't discovered the Internet and are wondering how to get online, pick up *Getting on the Internet*, new from CliffsNotes. You'll learn just what you need to make your online connection quickly and easily. See you at www.cliff-notes.com!

CHAPTER 1
SCOPING OUT ONLINE INVESTING

IN THIS CHAPTER

- Looking at online investing and traditional investing
- Thumbing through the different types of investments
- Checking off the equipment you need to get started

Are you ready to take control of your own investments by going online? You can save hundreds or even thousands of dollars in commission costs each year by opening an online brokerage account. You can also enjoy the flexibility and sense of independence you get by managing your own assets.

Online investing, though once perceived as fast-paced and risky, is now viewed as the mainstream, economical investing alternative. Even if you have a long-established, comfortable relationship with a trusted broker (who happens to be your brother-in-law), online investing is a trend you can't afford to ignore.

Comparing Online Investing to Traditional Investing

Online investing reduces the money you have to pay a broker to trade securities. You can also react to market conditions more quickly because you don't have to contact your broker to execute a trade. However, when you take charge of your own investing strategy, you need to start doing your own homework to substitute for the research and advice you get (or are supposed to get) from a broker.

What's different about online investing?

Both online investing and traditional investing are supposed to make you money. You have to decide for yourself whether you profit more handsomely from doing your own online research and trading or from the services of a broker. Table 1-1 helps you compare the online investing medium to traditional investing.

Table 1-1: Comparing Traditional Investing and Online Investing

Traditional Investing	Online Investing
The phone is your most important investment tool.	The computer is your most important investment tool.
Investors buy and sell makes the purchase on the investor's behalf.	Investors buy and sell securities themselves by using a computer to access the brokerage's Web site.
Investors pay their brokers a commission on each trade.	Investors pay their brokerage a fee that's normally a fraction of a full-service broker's fee.
Brokers monitor your portfolio all day long, sometimes calling to inform you of a danger or opportunity.	You monitor your own portfolio by using a variety of online methods.
Careful research and planning is necessary.	Careful research and planning is necessary.

Evaluating the role of the broker versus the computer

Before you give your broker the boot so that you can go online, evaluating the services you actually get for the cost of your broker's commission is a good idea. You may decide that you're getting some benefits from using a broker that you're not ready to forgo.

You may feel more comfortable, for example, relying on the advice of an experienced broker who monitors the market all day (while you're away from your computer doing other things). And your broker has the lines of communication to gauge what other brokers are feeling and advising their clients to do.

Sometimes dealing with a broker is more practical than using a computer. For example, you may like to pick up the phone occasionally to ask a question and talk to the same person each time. Or, if you travel frequently (particularly overseas), you may not always have access to a computer.

Online investing and traditional brokerage services aren't mutually exclusive. You may even consider maintaining more than one kind of account, giving you access to differing levels of service.

Brokers are licensed and registered with the Securities and Exchange Commission (SEC) to regulate the quality of the advice they give you. Brokers have to pass a rigorous test to receive a Series 7 license. The SEC can discipline brokers who fail to follow SEC rules and standards in giving advice. The SEC cannot discipline *you* for failing to properly research your own online investments. By investing online, you assume the responsibility *and* the risk.

Comparing speed

Online investing provides you with a fast communication medium for buying and selling investments and for keeping up with the market. After you open an account, you can place an order to buy and sell stocks in less than 60 seconds.

Several Web sites also provide you with price quotes to help you optimize the timing of your transactions. Web site quotes are updated at various intervals, depending on the Web site. Intervals range from daily, to every 15 to 20 minutes, or even so-called *real-time* quotes that appear on your screen within seconds of a market movement. Most brokerages offer real-time quotes, but they generally charge you a fee to access them.

Tip

The Raging Bull Web site at www.ragingbull.com (shown in Figure 1-1) offers a real bargain for investors who want access to real-time quotes without paying an extra fee. In exchange for providing certain information about yourself and your investment needs, you can receive free access to the Raging Bull real-time quotes. (You need to weigh the slight loss of privacy against the benefit of having access to the most current quote information.)

Figure 1-1:   Raging Bull offers free real-time quotes to registered users.

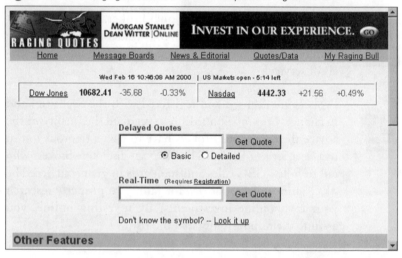

Unfortunately, the speed of online investing induces some investors to trade impulsively. Speed can be dangerous for investors who react before researching investment decisions or for those who don't have a grasp of basic investing concepts. (Chapter 2 tells you what you need to know and how to prepare before going online.)

Learning investment basics

Both online and traditional investing require an understanding of financial markets, products, and basic principles of investing. The National Association of Investors Corporation (NAIC) is a not-for-profit organization that maintains a

Web site devoted to educating investors. You can learn how to develop a sound investment strategy from the NAIC Web site located at www.better-investing.org.

Figure 1-2 shows a page on the NAIC Web site that explains basic investment principles. Access this page by clicking <u>Home</u> ☞ <u>NAIC Education</u> ☞ <u>four basic investing principles</u>.

Figure 1-2:   Web site for a not-for-profit organization devoted to educating investors.

NAIC's Four Easy Investment Principles

NAIC principles for investing are basic and have been producing financial success for individuals and investment clubs for over 45 years.

The four basic principles are:

1. Invest regular sums of money once a month in common stock. This helps you obtain a lower average cost on your investments.
2. Reinvest all earnings, dividends and capital gains. Your money grows faster if earnings are reinvested. This way, compounding of your money is at work for you.
3. Buy growth stocks--companies whose sales and earnings are increasing at a rate faster than the industry in general. They should have good prospects for continued growth, or in other words, they should be stronger, larger companies five years from now.
4. Invest in different industries. Diversification helps spread both risk and opportunity.

Finding out about minimum balances, fees, and costs

Traditionally, brokerage firms have required a fairly substantial minimum balance to open an account — upwards of $1,000. Online brokerage firms tend to be far more liberal about minimum balance requirements. You can generally open online accounts with nominal minimum balances. Chapter 6 explains how you open an online account.

Each online brokerage firm has to post a schedule of all its commissions, fees, and service charges on its Web site. Online brokerage commissions and fees are almost always substantially lower than the costs associated with traditional full-service or discount brokers.

Lower online commissions and service fees are due in large part to lower overhead — fewer buildings to maintain and decorate to impress clients, and fewer brokers sitting in them. The competition of having so many brokerage firms posting their fee schedules on the Web also drives costs down. (Chapter 6 tells you more about how to compare fees and services for various online brokers.)

Scrolling Through Online Investment Options

When people think of investing, they usually think of stocks. But one of the basic goals of sound investing is to accumulate a diverse portfolio. Your *portfolio* is your collection of assets, and it should include an array of investments with different levels of risk — maintaining this variety is called *diversification*. (I further explain the principle of diversification in Chapter 2.)

Stocks and the stock market

Buying a stock in a company instantly gives you a stake in its future performance. Generally, the stock of profitable companies appreciates, and you may even get to share in the profits via a dividend distribution. You also get to vote for the people who manage the company. You can only buy stock in *a publicly traded company.* A publicly traded company offers stock to members of the public on a stock exchange as opposed to being privately owned (as I discuss in Chapter 3).

Being online can be a real advantage when you invest in the stock market. You can react to the market more quickly by using brokerage services that you can find only on the Web.

For example, the Datek Online Web site, located at
www.datek.com, allows you to select which stocks you
want to monitor continuously on your screen throughout the
day. This Web site, shown in Figure 1-3, uses a billboard format on which numbers are constantly changing to give you
real-time quotes for the investments you monitor.

Figure 1-3:   Datek's streaming window.

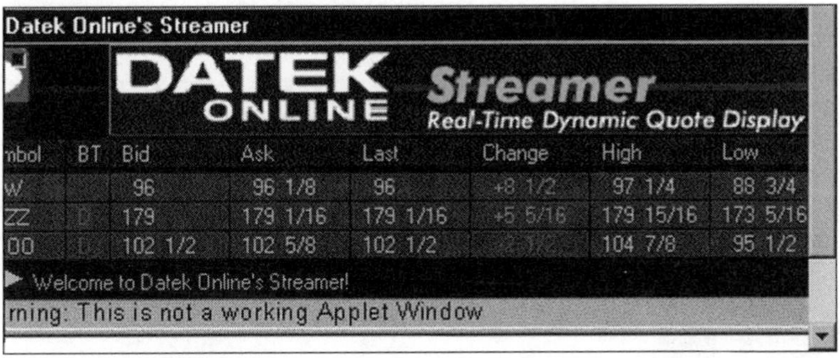

Bonds

Having some bonds in your portfolio is a good idea to hedge
your bets just in case the stock market ever takes a prolonged
dip. You can't have a diversified portfolio without including
some bonds. Bonds are essentially loans you make to government entities or to private companies that are repaid at a
predetermined rate of interest.

Government entities, as well as private companies, issue
bonds. When you purchase a bond, you lend money to the
bond issuer, who pays interest on the loan at a predetermined
interval and repays the principle at the end.

The success of your bond investments depends on whether
the interest you receive on the bond exceeds the income you
may have earned through other types of investments. For
example, assume you're receiving 6 percent interest on a
bond, while other bond investments are paying 7 percent.
Your 6 percent investment is profitable but has a cost to you
in terms of lost opportunity.

You can research, select, and purchase bonds online. By logging on to a free Web site such as www.bondsonline.com shown in Figure 1-4, you can research the types of bonds currently available and the ratings given to them by an agency called Standard & Poor's. You can also find out about new bonds that are going to be issued and get real-time quotes for ones currently on the market.

Figure 1-4:   The Bonds Online Web site allows you to quickly research and compare hundreds of bonds.

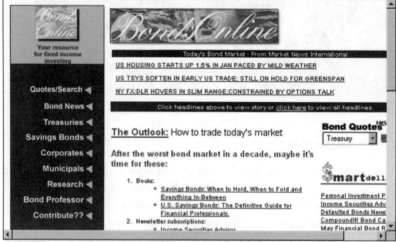

Bonds Online is a trademark of Bonds Online, Inc.

Mutual funds

Mutual funds provide you with the benefit of investing in many companies at the same time. A mutual fund is an array of stocks, bonds, and even cash that's managed by an investment company expert on behalf of a group of many investors. Instead of buying a share in a single company, you purchase a share of the fund. When you buy shares of a mutual fund, you own a portion of its assets along with all the other fund investors.

Literally thousands of funds are registered with the SEC. Mutual funds come in all shapes, sizes, and compositions.

For example, you can buy shares of an environmentally conscious fund or a high-tech fund.

A good starting point for mutual fund research is the Forbes Mutual Fund Information Center Web site that you can access by navigating to the Forbes home page (www.forbes.com) and clicking the mutual funds hyperlink. The site's searchable database, shown in Figure 1-5, allows you to compare over 5,500 mutual funds. (Try asking your broker to do that!)

Figure 1-5:   You can compare over 5,500 funds using a single Web site.

Enter fund name to research here

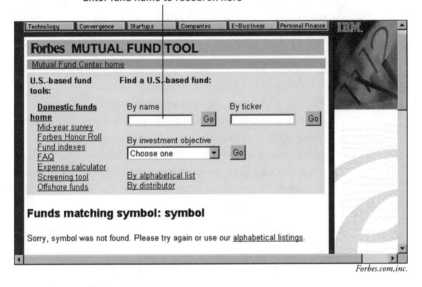

Forbes.com,inc.

Index funds

Index funds are a great way to ride the crest of the generally rising stock market without having to do a lot of research or put effort into diversifying your stock purchases. Expert analysts who use special computer programs to put together the index fund have already done that for you.

A *stock index* is a sampling of stocks used to measure the activity and strength of the stock market as a whole. An index fund tracks its stated index, for example, the S&P 500, and provides performance results similar to the performance of the index as a whole. The fund manager invests in all (or a large percentage) of the stocks that make up that particular index. The idea behind an index fund is that the fund mimics the index by including the same stocks the index analysts have chosen to represent the market. As the value of the stocks in the index rises or falls, so should your index fund.

Others

There are several other types of investments that most financial advisors agree don't belong in the portfolio of the beginning investor because of the high degree of risk and volatility associated with them.

Novice and risk-averse investors should avoid the following:

- **Options:** An option contract gives a speculator the right (but not the obligation) to buy or sell a stock at a given price on a future date called the strike date. If the stock price moves in the direction the speculator expects, then on the strike date, he or she can either buy the stock for less than the market price or sell it for more than the market price and earn a profit.

  But if the stock price doesn't perform as expected, then the right to buy or sell the stock becomes worthless (anyone can get a better price on the open market). The speculator loses the investment and receives nothing in return.

- **Commodities:** Speculators bet on the daily price of *commodities* (raw materials or foods such as cotton, gold, or even pork bellies) through contracts called *futures*. Futures contracts *obligate* speculators to buy or sell a specific amount of a commodity for a given price on the strike date. If speculators guess right, then they can buy below or sell above the market price (depending on the type of futures contract) and make money.

If they guess wrong, however, then they have to buy the amount of the commodity specified in the contract above the market price or sell that amount below the market price, possibly losing more than they invested — sometimes *much* more.

- **Hedge funds:** These are unregulated investment funds. Because they're unregulated, fund managers can invest in riskier and more speculative investments — such as options and futures.

Getting Started: A Checklist

Online investing allows you to replace your broker with a new type of investment advisor — your computer. But first you need to take inventory of your hardware and software to make sure you have the following:

- **Enough memory, processing speed, and disk storage space:** Select a computer that has the memory, processing speed, and storage space you need to run your financial and portfolio management software. The requirements for a particular software program appear on the Web site for the program or on the box if you're purchasing it off the shelf.

- **Modem:** A modem is the hardware device that allows your computer to communicate over standard telephone lines. Most computers come with modems that transmit data at a maximum rate of 56 Kbps.

- **Internet account:** Just as you need to open an account with your local telephone company to access the public telephone lines, you need to open an account with an Internet Service Provider (ISP) to access the Internet. You can usually find dozens of ISPs in your local phone book.

■ **Web browser:** Documents on the Internet are written using special languages such as HTML and Java. To read the materials on the Internet, you need to have a special software program on your computer called a *browser.*

Windows-based programs come with the Microsoft Internet Explorer software. You can also download Netscape Communicator software from the Internet by going to the Netscape Web site located at www.netscape.com.

■ **Personal finance software:** This type of software can help you track and analyze your investments more effectively. The most popular and widely used personal finance software is Intuit's Quicken.

If you don't think you're going to want to manage your checkbook and other accounts online, you may want to consider a program that's limited to portfolio management.

You can register to use portfolio management software that's located on a Web site (such as the NAIC Web site, at www.better-investing.org), or you can buy and install a program on your own PC.

CHAPTER 2

MAKING THE ONLINE DECISION

IN THIS CHAPTER

- Navigating the thousands of investing Web sites
- Getting comfortable with the basic principles for online investing
- Understanding investment risk
- Doing a self-assessment

The real secret of profitable online trading is preparation. Your success depends mostly on what you do before you make a trade. In this chapter, you learn how to wade through financial data at the more than 10,000 Web sites devoted to online investing. You also apply basic principles of investing to online trading and identify factors every investor should consider when analyzing a potential investment.

Navigating Online Investment Web Sites

Even the most basic Internet query can turn up hundreds of online investing Web sites purporting to give you hot tips and insights you can't get elsewhere. If you turn on your television, you're confronted with commercials telling you that you are losing out by failing to check out yet more investing sites. Where do you start?

Online investing requires researching and evaluating information on the Web — not just clicking your mouse to make a stock trade. But you certainly can't read all the information that's available online. There's just too much information.

Here are a few pointers for sifting through the proliferation of Web sites for golden nuggets of online investing wisdom:

■ **Don't pay for information you can get for free.** Does the Web site ask you to subscribe? Take advantage of trial subscriptions offered by many reputable organizations, such as the Lycos Investing site (`www.lycos.com/lycos/quote.asp`) shown in Figure 2-1, to evaluate any subscription you're considering. Determine if the information is already available to you someplace else for free. For example, the inside financial scoop on most companies is available for free in their annual reports. Free stock quotes are on the Web site of each exchange and the NASDAQ.

Figure 2-1: Many reputable Web sites offer free trial subscriptions and sample publications.

■ **Look for relevant information.** Trying to read everything online about an investment isn't a good use of your time. Your goal is to look at *relevant* information — such as the current price, historical value, past profits, and management capabilities. (In the section titled "Getting the Answers," later in this chapter, I tell you what information to research and where to get it.)

■ **Look for objective information.** To determine if a Web site is offering objective information, you need to ask a few basic questions. Is the Web site trying to sell you a subscription? Does anyone get a commission from investments they're advising you to look at? Who's paying for site advertising? The presence of the profiteers can be subtle! With so much information on the Web, bypass the promotional stuff in favor of objective information.

■ **Take advantage of not-for-profit Web sites.** The advice that analysts offer is interesting, but the most enduring investing principles and strategies are available for free. Several not-for-profit organizations, such as the American Association of Individual Investors at `www.aaii.com` (see Figure 2-2) and the National Association of Investors Corporation at `www.betterinvesting.org`, maintain Web sites devoted solely to educating investors. These organizations offer memberships for a nominal cost, which entitle you to use all areas of their Web sites as well as other support services they provide.

Basic Online Investing Principles

You can't help but be interested in hearing what the analyst *du jour* has to say about how to make a killing in the stock market. But avoid the impulse to allow a piece of news or an opinion to send you scampering to your computer to buy or sell stocks.

Online investors may occasionally guess right about the movement of a particular stock and succeed in buying low and selling high over a short time period. Bear in mind, however, that the vast majority of investors who try to use the Internet to anticipate the stock market on a day-to-day basis (the *beat-the-market* approach) lose money in the long run. A day-to-day trading approach is also more time-consuming and stressful.

Figure 2-2: Not-for-profit organizations maintain Web sites devoted to educating investors.

You should, instead, according to the NAIC, focus on using your computer to find investments that you reasonably expect to double in value over a five-year period. The NAIC recommends that you stick to the following four basic online investing principles.

Principle #1: Invest online systematically

Online investing should never be done on impulse. Snap decisions can be a real danger, because after you establish an account, you can buy or sell any stock in less than 60 seconds. And thousands of Web sites offer you hot tips and advise you to purchase something that is currently "undervalued" or "about to take off."

The NAIC recommends that you invest "regular sums of money once a month in common stock" rather than taking the beat-the-market approach. This systematic approach encourages discipline. More importantly, systematic investing increases your odds of making a profit through the benefit of *dollar cost averaging.*

Dollar cost averaging presumes that the market goes up and down over day-to-day and month-to-month periods. But over a period of several years, dollar cost averaging assumes that the trend is upward. The assumption that the market (as a whole, not necessarily stock by stock) is likely to rise in value over longer time periods is borne out by the past performance of the stock market.

If you purchase large amounts of stock in a particular month and the market goes down two months later, you've lost money. (And you've agonized over your big purchase and the stock's subsequent decline.) However, if you systematically purchase a small amount of stock each month, you can actually *benefit* from declines in the market. In the months when stock prices are down, you buy at a lower price, which, barring fundamental problems at the company, is a bargain.

By making a commitment to buy, you don't need to stay glued to your computer screen, biting your nails over when to buy and when to sell. Instead, you systematically identify good stocks and make regular purchases each month without worrying about short-term fluctuations.

Principle #2: Diversify your online investments

Fortunes are made and lost on the principle of diversification. Diversification means that you invest in different types of industries and types of investments instead of just one. This principle is especially important in the fast-paced environment of online investing.

Diversification, according to the NAIC, "spreads both risk and opportunity." For example, if your technology stocks suddenly take a nosedive due to the outbreak of an insidious global computer virus, you'll be glad you haven't risked everything and chose to diversify your stock portfolio to include manufacturing, retail, and other types of stocks. If the entire stock market is affected by the computer virus, you benefit even further if you've diversified to include bonds in your portfolio as well.

Principle #3: Reinvest your online profits

You can accelerate the process of building your wealth without increasing the time and effort you spend online. Reinvesting your dividends, interest, and the profit you derive from selling an investment compounds your earnings. *Compounding* occurs when you earn profits on your profits, and it makes your assets grow exponentially.

Principle #4: Select online investments for long-term growth

Day trading is a strategy where investors try to profit from short-term daily fluctuations in the stock market. According to *USA Today*, only one out of every five day traders makes money.

Financial experts agree that you should focus on long-term growth potential. You probably see the wisdom in purchasing only those stocks that you believe have the potential to double in value over the next five years.

The problem is that when you're investing online, it's easy to become influenced by temporary market fluctuations as opposed to the long-term growth indicators on which you need to focus. Continuous quotes scrolling across your screen showing your stock going down can make even the most committed investor jittery about staying the course. The next section of this chapter gives you a few pointers on how to research the long-term potential of a stock.

Focusing on purchasing investments that you intend to hold for a year or more provides important tax benefits as well. If you hold an investment for 12 months or longer before you sell it, the profits are taxed at favorable capital gains rates. Capital gains rates are substantially lower than regular tax rates.

Getting the Answers

As an online investor looking for profits over the long haul, you need to ignore much of the day-to-day market activity. You want to bypass trendy Web sites offering so-called *hot tips* and use that computer of yours to do some *real* research.

For a stock or mutual fund, you need to ask whether you can reasonably expect your investment to double in five years, as recommended by the NAIC. For a bond investment, you're looking to strike a balance between high interest income and the stability and diversification you expect to get from adding bonds to your portfolio. (In Chapter 5, I explain how riskier bonds pay higher interest and how to assess this trade-off.)

The most useful Web sites for evaluating the three major types of investments — stocks, mutual funds, and bonds — are summarized in Table 2-1. I tell you more about what you can expect to find on these Web sites, and how to use them, in Chapters 3 through 5, which deal specifically with each type of investment.

Table 2-1:   Best Web Sites for Online Investment Research

Investment Type	URL	What You Can Find
Stocks	www.marketguide.com	Stock screening software that allows you to screen stocks based on 20-75 factors you select.
Stocks	www.investor-ama.com	Links to thousands of articles, and a searchable database you can use to research articles on a specific company .
Stocks	www.prars.com	You can order free copies of almost any company's annual report, as I discuss in Chapter 3.

(continued)

Table 2-1: *(continued)*

Investment Type	URL	What You Can Find
Stocks	www.better-investing.org	This is the Web site of the NAIC, a not-for-profit organization devoted to educating consumers about investing in stocks. You can find lots of straight talk and good advice about investing. You can even find links for joining investment clubs that allow you to brainstorm with other investors.
Stocks	www.cnbc.com	You can get free stock quotes and access to a ticker symbol look-up service on this Web site.
Mutual Funds	www.ici.org	You can download informative publications covering the basics of mutual fund investing from this not-for-profit site.
Mutual Funds	www.quicken.com	You can use the Quicken mutual fund finder to screen for mutual funds that meet your specific criteria.
Mutual Funds	www.micropal.com	This Web site contains an enormous searchable database of mutual fund information. It allows you to screen funds based on criteria such as performance, industry sector, and capitalization of fund manager.
Mutual Funds	www.standard-poor.com www.nasdaq.com www.dowjones.com	Provides information about how stocks are selected for indexes that are used as the basis for index fund investments.

Investment Type	URL	What You Can Find
Mutual Funds	www.quicken.com	Provides a searchable database for bond funds, and other types of mutual funds.
Mutual Funds	www.social invest.org	This is a not-for-profit Web site that provides information and a searchable database for funds meeting social objectives.
Mutual Funds	www.morningstar.com	Offers commentaries and analysis of various mutual funds.
Bonds	www.standard poor.com www.moodys.com	Both the Standard & Poor's and Moody's Web sites maintain comprehensive bond rating systems. A trip to their Web sites helps you understand how the rating systems work.
Bonds	www.bondagent.com/guests	This Web site is dedicated to providing information on bonds that pay interest that is tax-free at either the federal or state level.
Bonds	www.investing inbonds.com	Provides information and checklists for the beginning investor.
Bonds	www.publicdebt.treas.gov	You can use this Web site to research, evaluate, and purchase U.S. government bonds.

Doing a Self-Assessment

Investment strategies are as different as fingerprints. You need to do a pretty thorough self-assessment to resolve the following issues:

■ **How much can you afford to invest?** If you have a lot of credit card or other high-interest debt, your best investment may be to pay it off first. Paying off a credit card with an interest rate of 22 percent gives you an automatic annual 22 percent return on the money you spend toward paying it off.

■ **When and how often will you invest?** Weekly, monthly or annually? Investing incrementally and systematically over time (for example, each month) reduces risk attributable to market fluctuations. You'll purchase some investments at market highs and others during a decline. With systematic, smaller investments, you don't have to worry about the day-to-day or month-to-month fluctuations.

■ **What are your investment goals?** NAIC guidelines recommend that you seek to double your investments every five years in working toward larger goals such as college savings or retirement.

■ **What is your tolerance for risk?** Risk is inherent in all investments. Many investors, when confronted with unanticipated risks, start selling assets in a panic. This reaction compounds their losses. The best approach to assessing your personal risk tolerance is to identify the direst worst-case scenario you can psychologically and financially handle and not invest in a way that would increase your losses beyond that.

■ **What industries and types of investments should you include in your portfolio?** Diversification is an important step toward minimizing risks. It means that you hold as many varieties of investments purchased at as many different times as possible in your portfolio. You should attempt to diversify the types of industries and sectors of the economy in which you invest, the types of securities you purchase (for example, include bonds and mutual funds as well as stocks), and the timing of your investment purchases.

CHAPTER 3
RESEARCHING STOCKS ONLINE

IN THIS CHAPTER

- Screening stocks online
- Reading what the online analysts have to say
- Preparing your own analysis
- Brainstorming with other investors

Where do the hottest stock tips come from? The people with the coolest heads — and the most background information — generate them. And truly hot tips don't come from people with ulterior profit motives or newsletter subscriptions to sell. In fact, you may be your own best tipster. This chapter gives you pointers on how to separate the hot tips from the lukewarm losers when it comes to picking stocks.

Diversifying Your Portfolio

Diversification is free insurance. It doesn't protect you against every conceivable risk, but experts unanimously agree that your online stock screening criteria should promote a diversified portfolio. A diversified portfolio insures you against market swings affecting one company, industry, or economic sector.

Diversifying according to sector

With a diversified portfolio, the value of your entire stock portfolio doesn't plummet if a single industry in which you own stock is on the skids. To diversify, purchase stocks that represent different components of the economy, called sectors. A *sector* is a category of related industries.

You don't need to buy stocks in every economic sector — just a healthy array of unrelated industries. According to the NAIC, you can have a well-diversified portfolio by purchasing stocks in just a half a dozen sectors. Economists all use different criteria for categorizing businesses into sectors. Table 3-1 provides a list of 12 sectors listed on the Market Guide Web site (go to www.marketguide.com and click the What's Hot link) and examples of the industries they represent.

Table 3-1: Twelve Sectors of the U.S. Economy

Sector	Examples of Types of Industries Included in Sector
Technology	Computers, software, communications equipment, office equipment
Consumer cyclical	Appliances, recreational products, furniture, apparel
Services	Retail, business services, rental and leasing, printing and publishing, hotels, waste management
Energy	Coal, oil, and gas
Capital goods	Construction, supplies, and fixtures
Transportation	Trucking, railroads, airline, air courier
Utilities	Water, electric, natural gas
Health care	Biotechnology and drugs, medical facilities, medical supplies
Basic materials	Paper products, forestry, chemicals, metal mining, plastics, rubber, gold and silver
Financial	Investment services, insurance, savings & loans

Sector	Examples of Types of Industries Included in Sector
Consumer	Livestock, tobacco, food processing, fish, non-cyclical livestock, beverages
Conglomerates	Large diversified companies (such as ITT Industries, Inc., or TRW, Inc.)

Diversifying according to size

Small companies' stock prices tend to be more volatile than those of large companies. Even within the same industry, stocks of companies of different sizes tend to increase and decrease at different times. When large-company stocks are up, small-company stocks may be down, and vice versa.

A company's size is determined by its market capitalization, or *market cap*. Market cap is determined by multiplying the current price per share by the number of shares of the company's outstanding stock.

The three levels of market cap are as follows:

- **Small cap:** Less than $500 million
- **Mid cap:** $500 million to $5 billion
- **Large cap:** Greater than $5 billion

At least half your online portfolio should be made up of mid-cap stocks, and the remaining half should be split equally between small- and large-cap stocks.

Screening Your Stocks

How do smart, savvy (and wealthy) investors pick a stock? Invariably, they identify criteria for the types of stocks they want to own. Then they decide which stocks meeting those criteria are good buys. The process of coming up with a list of stocks that meet your personal investment criteria is called *screening*. Online research beats any traditional investing approach cold when it comes to screening stocks.

Creating a checklist of stock screening criteria

Investing philosophies are as controversial as political views. When it comes to predicting which stocks will double in value over the next five years, two mainstream "parties" exist.

The NAIC approach recommends that you focus on past performance and current ratios. The second school of thought is that you should mainly look for companies with undervalued share prices relative to the assets that appear on their financial statements. Both schools of thought rely on screening criteria to identify stocks that fit with their approach.

You can screen stocks by using software designed for the purpose or by using statistical information from a source such as the *Value Line Investment Survey*.

The *Value Line Investment Survey* is a publication that you can pay to subscribe to at www.valueline.com. You can also use *Value Line* for free at your local public library. *Value Line* contains information on over 1,700 stocks, and it ranks them according to safety, stability, earnings predictability, and other factors. The *Value Line* rating system is highly regarded by financial experts.

Table 3-2 shows a few of the most widely considered stock-screening criteria.

Table 3-2:   Stock Screening Criteria

Criterion	What It Means
Current Price	The price for which a share of the stock is currently selling.
Price Earnings Ratio	Stock price divided by earnings per share (a low figure may indicate that the company is undervalued).
Return on Assets	After-tax income divided by the total amount of assets (a measure of management's effectiveness).
Return on Equity	Income divided by total shareholders' equity (a measure of management's effectiveness).
Return on Investment	After-tax income divided by total assets and long-term debt (a measure of management's effectiveness).
Beta	A measure of the volatility of the company's stock price relative to the market as a whole.
Book Value Per Share	The total amount of shareholders' equity divided by the number of shares of outstanding stock.
Current Ratio	The ratio of current assets divided by current liabilities.
Dividend Rate Share	The total amount of dividends per per share expected to be paid over the next 12 months.
Yield	Annual dividend for a share of stock divided by current stock price (expressed as a percentage).
Market Capitalization	The current share price multiplied by the current number of shares outstanding.
Earnings per Share	Total corporate earnings divided by the number of shares outstanding.
High and Low Selling Price of Stock	The highest and lowest stock selling price in the last six months.

Taking advantage of online stock screening software

Online screening technology can really save you time and help you make money. If you spend hours researching individual stocks one-by-one to see if they meet your criteria, you won't have a life. Fortunately, as an online investor, you have access to free powerful software that allows you to simultaneously screen hundreds of stocks based on 20 to 75 different factors.

Using the screening software

Two types of powerful screening software are available to you on the Market Guide Web site at www.market-guide.com free of charge. An online version, called NetScreen (see Figure 3-1), allows you to screen stocks using up to 20 different factors. The downloadable version, Stock Quest, lets you screen for stocks using up to 75 preselected criteria after you install the program on your PC.

When you're online, you can immediately begin screening stocks using NetScreen. Here's how it works:

1. Go to the Market Guide Web site, located at www.marketguide.com and click the <u>Screening</u> link to access the Net Watch software.

2. Click the Add button to bring up the NetScreen Criterion Builder window shown in Figure 3-2.

Figure 3-1: The main window for the free NetScreen online software.

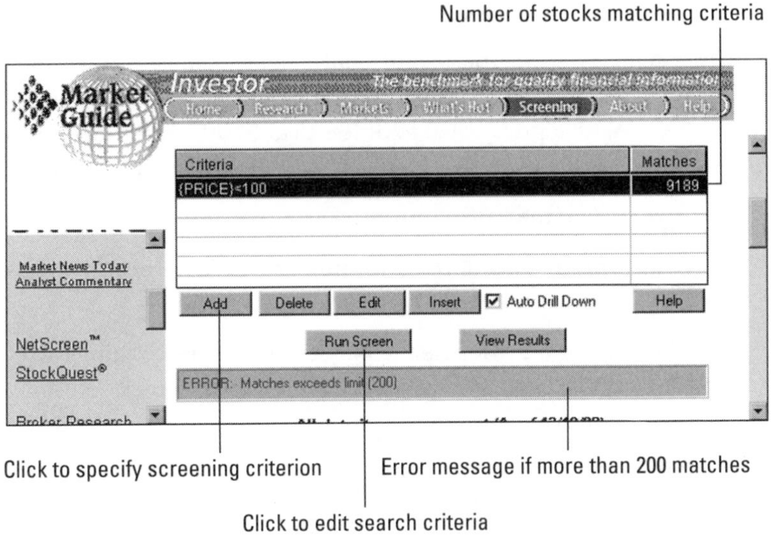

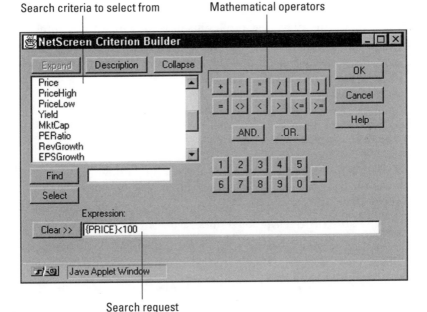

Number of stocks matching criteria

Click to specify screening criterion

Error message if more than 200 matches

Click to edit search criteria

Figure 3-2: Use the NetScreen Criterion Builder window to select search criteria.

Search criteria to select from

Mathematical operators

Search request

3. In the Variables field, select an option (such as Price) and click the Select button.

4. Click a mathematical symbol (called an operator), such as <, >, or =. For example, if you want to research stocks with a price equal to or less than $100, click the buttons until {PRICE}<=100 shows up in the Expression field.

5. Click the Select button.

6. Specify additional screening criteria by repeating Steps 2–5.

7. Click OK to close the NetScreen Criterion Builder window after you finish identifying all your stock-screening criteria.

8. Click the Run Screen button to generate a list of companies that match your criteria.

9. Click the View Results button to view a list of the names of stocks that meet your criteria in the Screening Results window.

You can't view the results of your search if the number of matching stocks is more than 200. If you come up with more than 200 matching stocks, click the Edit button to narrow your search criteria.

10. Click the name of any company to view a Company Snapshot report with more information about the company.

The NetScreen software program meets the needs of most investors. But you can also take a bit of extra time and download the more robust StockQuest program for free. It's available on the Market Guide Web site by going to 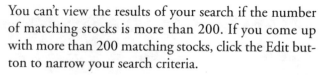www.marketguide.com and clicking <u>Home</u> ☞ <u>Screening</u> ☞ <u>StockQuest</u>. The StockQuest program offers you the following additional advantages:

- A total of 75 screening factors

- The ability to view a list with an unlimited number of companies that meet your search request (as opposed to the 200 NetScreen allows)

- Faster, more secure searching because the database is already downloaded onto your PC

If you choose to use StockQuest, you must update the database on your computer to keep it current. The Market Guide Web site offers daily StockQuest updates.

Both NetScreen and StockQuest are available to you absolutely free of charge. The Web site is financed by advertising and revenue Market Guide gets from selling its excellent database to other commercial Web sites.

Technical support for the Market Guide Web site could easily put the support services offered with most paid software products to shame. If you e-mail Market Watch a question, the support staff responds in about 24 hours and sends along a phone number to call in case you still have questions.

Going beyond the initial screening

The process of screening stocks is a preliminary exercise, not the final step in your analysis. Stock-screening software is intended to help you identify potential investments meeting your initial selection criteria, not to analyze the merits of a specific investment.

Accordingly, keep a couple of things in mind when you're initially screening stocks:

- **Web sites used for screening stocks (as opposed to actually trading them) are updated daily.** You should confirm information that could change during the course of the day (such as the purchase price) before you actually make a stock trade.

■ **Stock screening programs aren't analytical tools that predict the growth of individual stocks over the long term.** Rather, these programs help you find stocks that meet certain criteria *today*.

After you develop a short list of stocks that meet your initial criteria, use the resources that I discuss in the next section to thoroughly analyze each stock on your list for its five-year growth potential.

Evaluating the Stocks You've Screened

After you screen a list of finalists — all the stocks that meet your initial screening criteria — it's time to put those beauties under a microscope. You want to look for hidden flaws and profit-making potential.

Reading what the analysts have to say

You can't believe everything you read on the Web. If you do, you'll be broke in no time.

But certain Web sites, online newsletters, and so-called e-zines do merit your time and attention. These resources can help you narrow your focus when multiple stocks meet your criteria and you need to decide which ones you should pursue further. They can tell you what's happening in the real world beyond the four corners of the company's balance sheet.

The most helpful and comprehensive Web site to consult when looking for newsletters and online publications known as e-zines is www.investorama.com, as shown in Figure 3-3.

The Investorama Web site offers you a database of thousands of articles and over 12,500 links to other Web sites. You can search for the name of a company in which you're considering investing or do a keyword search describing the kinds of stocks that interest you. You're rewarded with a list of articles, newsletters, and commentaries that meet your search request.

The Investorama Web site is an ideal starting point whether you're looking to see what analysts have to say about a particular stock or you're interested in an overview of the market in general. The site's also a great place to find and order free samples of publications.

Figure 3-3: The Investorama Web site directs you to other online publications.

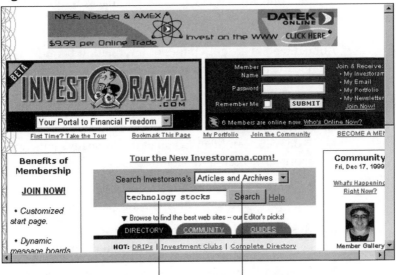

Enter search request   Select database

Reviewing a company's SEC filings

The government is on your side when it comes to getting information about publicly traded companies.

The Securities and Exchange Commission (SEC) requires all publicly traded companies to file an annual report. You can get the annual report from the company itself. Publicly traded companies are not only required to provide annual reports to investors (as I discuss in Chapter 2); they're required to file several other types of reports with the SEC during the year.

Looking at annual reports

If you're a shareholder of a company, then you automatically receive a copy of its annual report each year. If you're not a shareholder, you can either call the company to request an annual report or access it from the company's Web site. Usually the company has a hypertext link that you can click to download a copy of the report from the Web site.

Annual reports are gold mines of information because they include the following financial statements and information:

- **Income statement:** Discloses all of the company's earnings and profits for the year.

- **Balance sheet:** Identifies all of the company's long- and short-term assets and liabilities.

- **Statement of cash flows:** Tells you all of the company's sources for and uses of cash for the past year.

- **Research and development expenses:** Tells you a lot about where the company's headed in the future.

- **Overhead expenses:** High overhead expenses relative to total revenues can signal inefficient management or lagging markets for the company's products or services.

If you're researching several companies, you can order copies of all their annual reports at once using the Public Register Annual Report Service (PRARS) Web site located at www.prars.com. The PRARS Web site is a sort of clearinghouse for the distribution of annual reports. In exchange for entering certain information about yourself and completing a survey, PRARS will mail you copies of annual reports for the companies you've specified. You don't even have to pay postage!

Viewing other SEC filings

In addition to annual reports, the SEC requires companies with more than 500 investors and $10 million in assets to make other filings during the year. Some examples of required SEC filings include:

- **10-Q:** A quarterly form published three times a year to supplement the company's annual report.

- **8-K:** The SEC requires that this form be filed to provide notice of important financial events during the year that may affect shareholders' interests.

- **10-K:** A report that companies must file annually at the close of the fiscal year. It is a sort of unembellished annual report that lacks the fancy graphics and promotional hype included in the shareholders' annual reports.

You can search and download recent SEC filings for a company using the SEC Electronic Data Gathering and Retrieval Service (EDGAR). They're posted on the Web at `www.sec.gov/edgarhp` within 24 hours after SEC receives them.

An even more valuable government site than the EDGAR site is the FreeEdgar site, which collects several years' worth of SEC filings for each company and organizes them into comparative reports and charts. Using the data located at `www.freeedgar.com`, you can get a sense of a company's earnings, profits, and sales history over time. You can even sign up to receive e-mails from the FreeEdgar Web site alerting you each time a specified company has made a required filing.

Figure 3-4:   The SEC Electronic Data Gathering and Retrieval Service (Edgar) Web site.

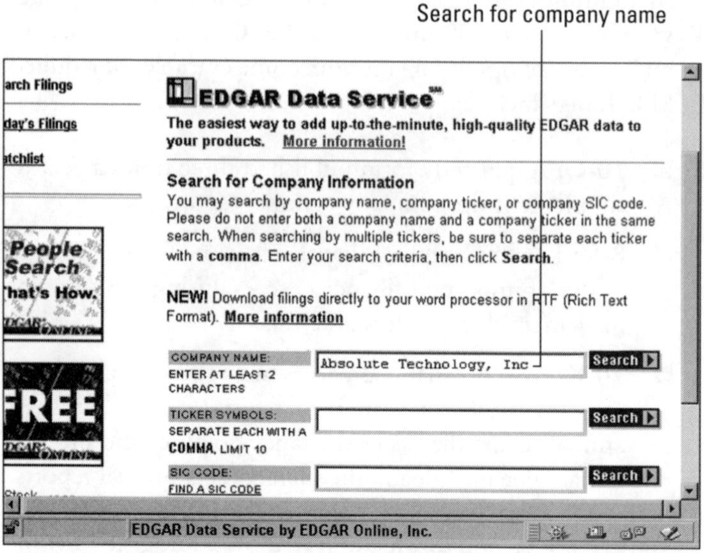

Search for company name

Comparative and historical data

The Value Line Investment Service (discussed earlier in this chapter) and the *Standard & Poor's Stock Guides* at www.stockinfo.standardpoor.com also provide comparative and historic company data. Unfortunately, neither of these services are free. You can either subscribe to them online or use them at your local public library.

Performing your own analysis

After you have a stack of annual reports, SEC filings, and other financial data from the Web, what do you do with it? How do you organize and evaluate it?

The NAIC Stock Selection Guide (SSG), is a tool that's been used and refined by investors for more than 50 years. A computerized version of the form is available to online investors with the NAIC Stock Analyst software. The NAIC recommends that you complete an SSG for every company in which you invest prior to purchasing its stock.

The SSG is divided into five sections. The SSG worksheet, when properly completed, tells you:

- Whether the company's historical sales, profit, and growth indicate a future upward trend.

- Whether the company is in the hands of good management.

- Whether the stock is likely to meet the NAIC goal of doubling in value within the next five years.

- If the company's stock is currently selling at a good price, based on historical price and profit data.

- Whether the risk, reward, and volatility of the stock (the *beta calculation*) are in an acceptable range.

The SSG takes some time to complete, but the result is well worth the effort. The Stock Selection Guide is a thorough analysis of factors carefully selected over five decades that's distilled to a relatively simple computerized worksheet you can complete yourself.

Brainstorming with Other Investors

If you're looking for someone to talk to about investments — without paying a commission — you can find plenty of sociable investors like yourself on the Web.

The NAIC has teamed up with Yahoo! to create online investment clubs. These clubs allow you to make cyber-buddies with whom you can chat online and pool investment knowledge. You can share investment strategies and results, and more importantly, your common interest in investing.

To take a look at a sample club, go to www.better-investing.org and click the Yahoo!Clubs hyperlink.

CHAPTER 4
RESEARCHING MUTUAL FUNDS

IN THIS CHAPTER

- Understanding mutual funds
- Finding out about bond funds
- Selecting mutual funds
- Buying mutual funds on the Web

Mutual funds are a gregarious type of investment — ideal for the type of person who wants the benefit of other people's expertise and research time. But even if you're a loner who prefers watching stock data stream across your screen, the impressive returns on many of the more successful mutual funds may make you come out of your shell and consider investing in the company of others.

Looking at How Mutual Funds Work

Would you rather buy a cake from an expert baker or make one from scratch? This is the sort of self-assessment you do when you choose whether to buy a mutual fund.

Mutual funds are ready-to-serve portfolios that contain a mix of stocks or bonds selected by a fund manager on behalf of a group of investors. These funds provide immediate investment diversification that you may not otherwise be able to afford. As always, convenience comes at a price — a variety of mutual fund fees. You also have lots of disclosures and performance data to evaluate. Fortunately, getting information about mutual funds is easy on the Web.

Learning mutual fund basics on the Web

Do you need to start with the basics when it comes to mutual funds? If so, you can visit a Web site dedicated to educating mutual fund novices.

The Investment Company Institute is a trade group for the mutual fund industry. The ICI has a financial interest in making sure consumers understand enough about mutual funds to feel comfortable buying them. To this end, it maintains a fact-filled Web site located at www.ici.org. If you click the <u>About Mutual Funds</u> link, as shown in Figure 4-1, you can view and download informative publications that cover all of the basics of mutual fund investing.

Figure 4-1:   This Web site is devoted to educating consumers about mutual funds.

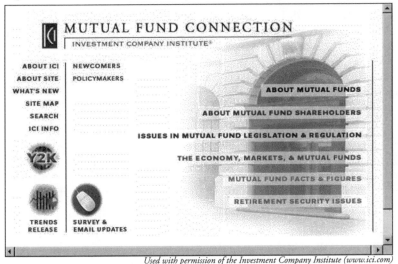

Used with permission of the Investment Company Institute (www.ici.com)

Reviewing a copy of the fund prospectus

Mutual funds are legally required to tell all when it comes to

■   Past performance of a fund

- The stocks, bonds, and other assets the fund holds
- Any fees associated with the fund

The document that reveals all of this information is called a *prospectus*.

You can usually download a prospectus from the fund's Web site, as shown in Figure 4-2.

Figure 4-2:   You can download a prospectus from most mutual fund Web sites.

Click to download prospectus

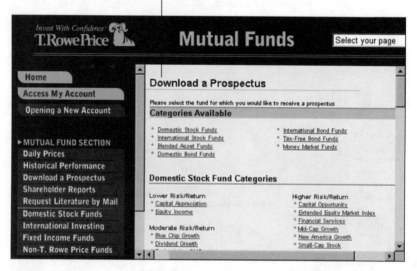

When you have the fund prospectus in hand, be sure to check its most recent *net asset value (NAV)*. The NAV is the total dollar value of all of the stocks and other securities owned by the fund, less expenses and divided by the number of outstanding fund shares. The NAV determines the price of individual shares of the fund.

Advantages and disadvantages of mutual funds

Mutual funds offer you great returns without the effort of shopping the Web for individual stocks and monitoring them. But they also have a few characteristics that can come back to haunt you.

On the whole, mutual funds are one of the safest, most effortless investments you can make. They offer the following benefits:

- **Professional management:** Mutual funds offer the professional expertise of sophisticated research analysts. You can search and view a list of funds that have a specific manager group by using the Standard & Poor's Micropal Web site at www.micropal.com. You can then review the performance of each manager's funds. I tell you more about the Micropal Web site and how to use it later in this chapter.

- **Instant diversification:** When you buy a fund, you buy an interest in a variety of stocks or bonds all at once rather than one at a time. This variety helps you meet the objective of a diversified portfolio. The fund prospectus (which you can download from the Web) tells you exactly which investments and sectors the fund holds.

- **Low entry costs:** You can invest as little as $250 in a mutual fund. You can use the Quicken.com Mutual Fund Finder (shown in Figure 4-3) at www.Quicken.com. Click Investing ☞ Fund Finder ☞ Popular Searches to search for funds that require investments of $250 or less or $500 or less.

- **Shareholder services:** The fund may offer check writing and other useful privileges. The fund's Web site usually promotes the services offered or includes a link so that you can e-mail a service person to find out about them.

Figure 4-3:   Quicken.com Mutual Fund Finder finds funds that require $250 or $500 to invest.

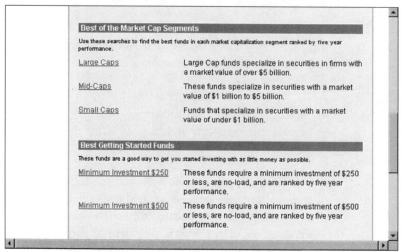

Best of the Market Cap Segments

Use these searches to find the best funds in each market capitalization segment ranked by five year performance.

Large Caps	Large Cap funds specialize in securities in firms with a market value of over $5 billion.
Mid-Caps	These funds specialize in securities with a market value of $1 billion to $5 billion.
Small Caps	Funds that specialize in securities with a market value of under $1 billion.

Best Getting Started Funds

These funds are a good way to get you started investing with as little money as possible.

Minimum Investment $250	These funds require a minimum investment of $250 or less, are no-load, and are ranked by five year performance.
Minimum Investment $500	These funds require a minimum investment of $500 or less, are no-load, and are ranked by five year performance.

Alas, there is no perfection in the world of investment, and mutual funds come saddled with inherent risks and baggage — just like any other opportunity. When investing in mutual funds, beware of the following:

■ **Fund managers who quit:** After you invest in a successful fund, you need to keep up with changes in management. For example, when star manager Peter Lynch ceased to manage the Fidelity Magellan fund in the 1990s, the value of the fund plummeted in relation to the stock market as a whole. You need to stay current and check out press releases announcing management changes. You can do so by reading the business section of your newspaper or looking at Web sites devoted to reporting investment news, such as Morningstar at www.morningstar.com, which I discuss later in this chapter.

■ **Loss of control over income tax issues:** Because the fund manager controls when stocks are sold, you may not always be able to defer your capital gains to years when they'll be taxed at a lower bracket or offset by other losses. (When you invest in individual stocks, you have the ability to control when you sell them.)

- **Misleading sales materials:** Advertising materials for funds may create an erroneous impression as to how the fund is actually managed and what investments are included. For example, a fund advertised as low risk may actually contain some pretty speculative stuff. Download a copy of the fund's prospectus and carefully review it to see what investments are actually included in the fund.

- **Hidden fees and costs:** Be sure you understand the fees associated with the fund, as disclosed in its prospectus. For example, a fund may charge a steep fee when you sell your shares.

Finding out about fund fees

Fortunately for you, the investor, all the information you need to know about a fund's fees is in one place — the prospectus. You should *never* invest in a fund without reading its prospectus.

After you download this document, scrutinize it carefully to ascertain your obligations for the following:

- **Load fee:** A load fee is a sales commission or charge you pay when you purchase a fund — generally around 5 percent. A *no-load* fund is one that does not require you to pay a commission or entry fee to invest in the fund. Most experts recommend no-load funds because a load fee immediately diminishes the amount of your investment.

- **12b-1 fees:** These are an alternative to load fees, used to compensate the person who sells the fund shares. A fund that charges a 12b-1 fee of less than .25 percent is considered a no-load fund.

■ **Redemption fees:** A redemption fee is often charged instead of a load fee. You pay this fee when you sell your mutual fund shares as opposed to when you buy into the fund. Typically, redemption fees decline over time to encourage you to hold onto your investment longer.

■ **Annual operating expenses and administrative costs:** These fees cover the basic costs of running the fund and are generally disclosed in the prospectus.

■ **Management fees:** These fees cover the costs of all those lawyers, accountants, and bookkeepers that make sure the fund complies with SEC rules. These, too, are disclosed and estimated in the fund prospectus.

Index funds (which I describe in Chapter 1) tend to charge lower fees than mutual funds. The reason for the lower fees is that after choosing stocks to mirror a given index, the funds require little management. Table 4-1 compares the performance of actively-managed funds with the performance of an S&P 500 stock index fund over a three-year period.

Table 4-1: Comparison of Mutual and Index Funds

Year	Increase in S&P 500 Over Previous Year	Increase in Average Actively Managed Fund Over Previous Year
1997	33.4%	24.6%
1998	28.6%	14.9%
1999	16.8%	19.5%

You can easily research index funds on the Web. The S&P's Web site is www.standardpoor.com — click the Standard & Poor's Index Services link. You can learn about the NASDAQ at www.nasdaq.com and the Dow Jones index at www.dowjones.com.

Considering Bond Funds

Stocks aren't all you'll find when you look at mutual funds. Bond funds offer professional management and diversification as well.

I discuss bonds more fully in Chapter 5, but a bond is basically an IOU from a government entity or corporation. You lend them the money, and they promise to pay you interest and principal. The riskier the bond investment, the higher the rate of interest. You can search for bond funds using the Quicken.com Web site at www.Quicken.com — click Investments ☞ Funds ☞ Popular Searches ☞ Bond Funds.

Bond fund managers offer professional expertise in balancing the risk and return of various types of bonds. There are three major differences between investing in a bond fund as opposed to purchasing an individual bond:

- **Diversification:** Bond funds offer you the advantage of a calculated mix of bond investments.

- **No fixed maturity date:** Individual bonds mature on a specific maturity date; bond funds do not mature. You decide when to sell your shares in a bond fund.

- **Fixed return:** When you purchase an individual bond, you know how much interest and principal is to be paid. When you buy into a bond fund, you may ultimately sell your shares at a gain or loss.

Finding a Fund That Meets Your Objectives

There's a smorgasbord of funds out there — and you need to have several types on your plate to be diversified.

You can use online fund-screening software such as the Standard & Poor's Micropal Web site at www.micropal.com

or the Quicken.com Mutual Fund Finder at www.quicken.com. At Quicken.com, click <u>Investing</u> ☞ <u>Fund Finder</u> ☞ <u>Popular Searches</u> to search for funds that represent the following categories:

- **Large-, mid-, and small-cap funds:** I discuss market capitalization of stocks — the price of a share of the company's stock multiplied by the number of outstanding shares — in Chapter 3. You can buy funds that specialize in large-, mid-, and small-cap stocks. Smaller capitalization correlates with higher risk and higher potential returns. The NAIC recommends that you select funds that specialize in a variety of market caps.

- **Aggressive growth funds:** Fund managers look for funds that have the highest growth potential. These stocks may be highly volatile, and you shouldn't invest in them if you may have to sell them at a time when the market is down. This type of fund may also include risky options and futures, which I discuss in Chapter 1.

- **High-performance funds:** These funds are less risk-oriented than aggressive growth funds, but the fund manager's main objective is still performance and growth.

- **Income funds:** These funds focus on companies with high dividend-paying potential.

- **Sector funds:** These funds purchase stocks in particular market sectors of the economy — such as health care or consumer goods. (I discuss sectors in Chapter 3.)

- **Tax-efficient funds:** These funds are managed so as to minimize taxable gains, and they include bond funds that invest in federal, state, and municipal bonds.

- **Socially conscious funds:** These funds invest to be consistent with investors' personal as well as financial objectives. I tell you how to use the Social Investment Forum Web site at www.socialinvest.org to research these funds later in the chapter.

- **International funds:** Managers of international funds undertake the complex research necessary to profit from overseas markets, which can be risky and complicated but can offer high returns.

- **Emerging market funds:** These funds are a high-risk version of international funds — specializing in Latin American, Middle Eastern, Asian, and other economies with volatile currencies.

- **Index funds:** Besides the Standard & Poor's Index, index funds are available that invest in small-cap index, international index, mid-cap index, bond index, and others.

Researching Mutual Funds on the Web

Literally hundreds of Web sites promote mutual funds and are devoted to fund screening and research. This section leads you straight to a few of the very best to help you get started.

Comparing funds: Standard & Poor's Micropal Web site

Standard & Poor's Micropal Web site at `www.micropal.com`, shown in Figure 4-4, is internationally acknowledged as the leading resource for fund information. This site monitors more than 38,000 funds around the world on a daily, weekly, and monthly basis. You can use the site to get information about a single fund, search for funds meeting your criteria, and compare the performance of funds identified by your specific search.

The Micropal home page contains a drop-down list of "live" databases. Each database contains a broad group of fund types, such as U.S. Mutuals or Offshore Funds. To use the Web site features, select a database from the drop-down menu. You can search only one database at a time.

Figure 4-4: The Micropal Web site is a comprehensive fund-screening source.

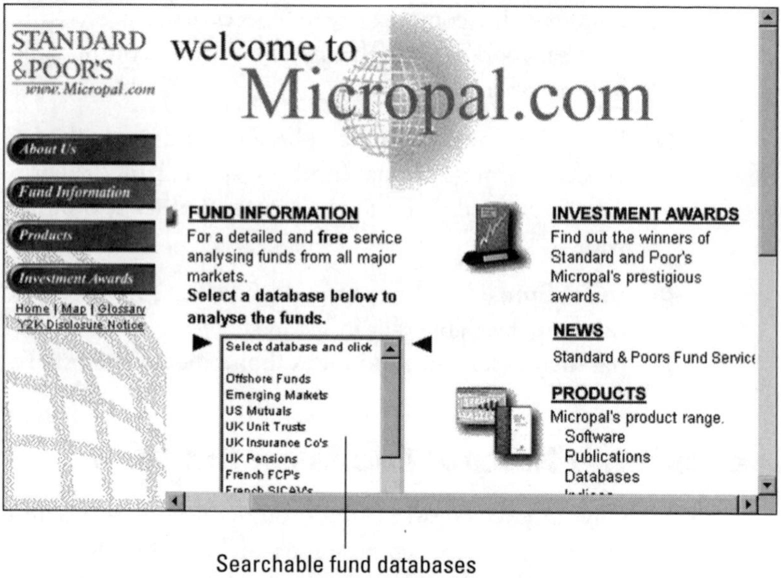

Searchable fund databases

After you select your database, an information page appears with some general information about the database. Click the <u>Click here to enter database and access fund information</u> link to view the Database Summary page, as shown in Figure 4-5. You can search the database by selecting one of the following options shown at the top of the database page:

■ **Management Groups:** If you select this search option, you can view a summary page with information about each fund management group (for example, Fidelity or Goldman Sachs). The information page for each management group tells you the contact information (such as the address, telephone number, and e-mail address) for the fund management group. This page also provides a drop-down menu listing each fund managed by the group, and you can select any fund to view detailed information about its historic performance, including graphs and charts.

■ **Performance Tables:** This search option allows you to compare the performance of similar types of funds that invest in similar sectors of the economy. You have the option of viewing fund performances over a period of six months to ten years. You can also export the tables into Excel.

■ **Fund Selector:** This feature allows you to search for funds that meet specific criteria such as the type of investment, the fund management group, and performance.

Using the Morningstar commentaries and fund screener

The Morningstar Web site funds area — click the Funds link at www.morningstar.com — offers you the benefit of commentaries and analysis as well as Web-based fund-screening software.

With Morningstar, you get a veritable library of mutual fund-related articles, as shown in Figure 4-6. You can read the opinions of lots of qualified experts, sometimes with opposing views, to help you make sense of all the raw numbers you get when you use fund-screening software.

Morningstar also offers online screening software that is simpler to use and offers less technical and comparative information than the Micropal Web site. This software may be easier to navigate for the beginner, although it's less comprehensive than the Micropal Web site.

Figure 4-5: The Micropal Database Summary page.

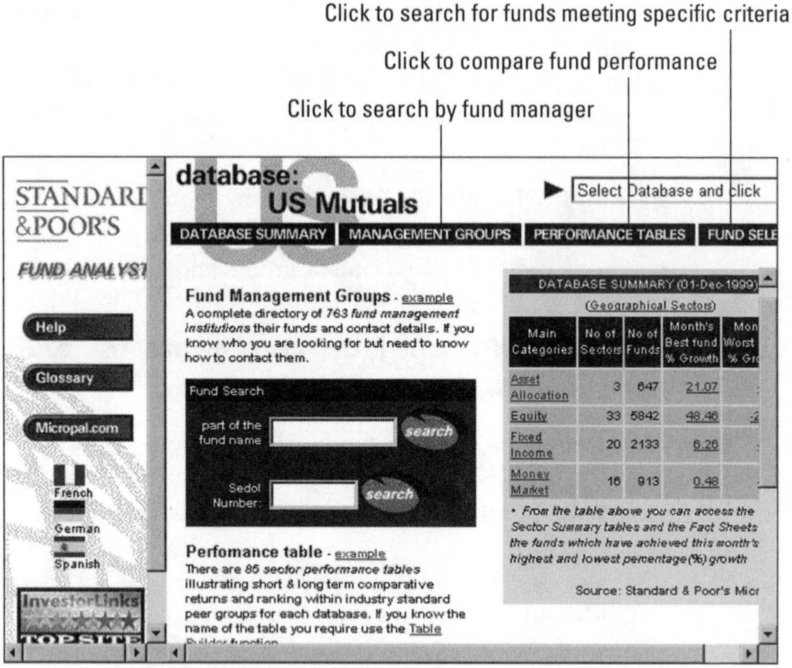

Click to search for funds meeting specific criteria

Click to compare fund performance

Click to search by fund manager

Finding socially conscious funds

Are you interested in putting your money where your principles are? If so, check out the Social Investment Forum Web site by going to www.socialinvest.org and clicking the Socially Responsible Mutual Funds link. This site, shown in Figure 4-7, is a great place to locate funds that meet your philosophical objectives. The Social Investment Forum is a not-for-profit organization devoted to socially responsible investing.

All funds included on the Web site must meet the Forum's objectives. You can screen for funds investing in companies that eschew things like alcohol, tobacco, firearms, and animal research. You can also screen the Forum-approved funds to determine past performance and the minimum investment they require.

Figure 4-6:   Morningstar provides a database of mutual fund articles.

www.morningstar.com

Figure 4-7:   The Social Investment Forum Web site is devoted to socially conscious mutual funds.

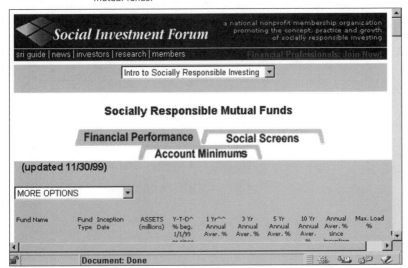

Buying Mutual Fund Shares Online

Have you finished your fund research and decided you'd like to buy some shares? You have two choices when it comes time to make the purchase. You can either get your funds through a brokerage or directly from a mutual fund company.

If you purchase your funds directly from the mutual fund company by accessing its Web site, you can save the cost of the brokerage commission that a broker may charge. You'll still be charged a transaction fee, but it's usually a lot less than a broker's commission. You can access a mutual fund Web site directly from many of the research sites discussed in this chapter, such as Quicken.com, Micropal, and the Social Investment Forum site.

CHAPTER 5

BUYING BONDS ONLINE

IN THIS CHAPTER

- ■ Understanding bond features
- ■ Assessing bond risk
- ■ Finding the best bond Web sites
- ■ Exploring bond buying strategies

Who says bonds are boring? True, bonds don't offer the cyber-thrills you get from watching stock prices soar and plummet on your computer screen, but bonds are especially important for the compulsively thrill-seeking online investor — they counteract riskier investments and still provide handsome profits.

You can't afford to ignore bonds — experts say bonds should make up at least 30 percent of your portfolio. This chapter explains how bonds buffer market risk and how to surf the Web for the ones with the most profit-making potential.

What's a Bond?

When you buy a bond, you're not buying a share of a company — you're issuing a loan and becoming a creditor of the company. Because you're not an owner, you don't get to vote or divvy up the profits. But, no matter how badly things go for the entity, you are entitled to receive your principal and an agreed-upon rate of return on your investment (as long as the issuer is solvent).

Looking at the bond issuer

The promise to repay is worth only as much as the credibility of the entity making the assurance. If an entity becomes insolvent, it may be unable to pay even its guaranteed obligations. For this reason, the most important characteristic of a bond is the issuing entity. The following types of entities issue bonds:

- **U.S. Treasury Department:** This debt is backed by the full faith and credit of the U.S. government and is literally the safest investment in the world.

- **Other U.S. government agencies:** From time to time, state and local government entities and agencies issue bonds to finance their projects and agendas. Examples include Federal National Mortgage Association (FNMA) Bonds and Student Loan Marketing Association (SLMA) bonds. Most (but not all) of these obligations are backed by the full faith and credit of the U.S. government. You need to ask the issuer to find out whether a bond is guaranteed by the U.S. government.

- **Corporations:** Corporations issue debt to finance their operations. They offer higher interest rates than government obligations because they're considered riskier.

- **State and local governments:** These agencies issue bonds to finance government projects and activities and use tax revenue or revenues generated by the project or activity financed to retire the bonds.

- **Foreign governmental entities:** These bonds are guaranteed by the governments of issuing countries, and they often offer a higher rate of return than U.S. obligations. However, they may be much riskier, depending upon the political climate and solvency of the issuing country.

Researching the issuer's credit rating

Bonds can be the cornerstones of your portfolio, offering you security and stability when the stock market's in a panic. Or they can literally be what investors call junk. *Junk bonds* are issued by financially shaky companies that offer higher-than-market interest rates because they absolutely can't get credit elsewhere. Junk bonds are considered *very* risky.

Just like you, bond issuers are given a credit rating. A poor credit rating affects their ability to get credit. One of the great benefits of being online is that you can look up the credit rating of a bond issuer in a matter of minutes.

The two most respected bond rating services are Standard & Poor's at www.standardpoor.com and Moody's at www.moodys.com. Both maintain their own alphabetic rating system, summarized in Table 5-1.

Only bonds having a Standard & Poor's rating of BBB or Moody's rating of Baa or better are considered investment quality bonds.

Table 5-1:   Investment Grade Bonds

Credit Risk	Moody's	Standard & Poor's
Highest Quality	Aaa	AAA
Very Strong	Aa	AA
Strong	A	A
Medium Grade	Baa	BBB

Non-investment grade bonds may have a place in your portfolio, but only in moderation. Invest in them sparingly. They don't have the same portfolio-stabilizing effect as higher grade bonds and, in fact, add a significant element of risk. Table 5-2 explains the available grades of non-investment grade bonds.

Table 5-2: Non-investment Grade Bonds

Credit Risk	Moody's	Standard & Poor's
Potentially Speculative	Ba	BB
Speculative	B	B
Highly Speculative	Caa	CCC
Most Speculative	Ca	CC
Danger of Imminent Default	C	C
In Default	-	D

The best source to get information about bond credit ratings is the Bonds Online Web site at www.bonds-online.com. This Web site allows you to search for bonds based on type, maturity date, interest rate, and other factors. You can view a list of bonds that meet your criteria and see both the Standard & Poor's and Moody's rating for each bond.

Taking inflation into account

An insidious, creeping threat to your bond portfolio is inflation. Because bonds pay a fixed rate of interest, rising interest rates and inflation can drive down your purchasing power. If you have a well-diversified portfolio, your stocks and other equity investments should rise in value to offset your losses from inflation. Additionally, in 1997, the U.S. Treasury began to offer inflation indexed notes, which I discuss later in this chapter in the section titled "Visiting the U.S. Treasury Web site."

Inflation and interest rates also determine how much a bond is worth on the secondary market. The *secondary market* consists of bonds sold after they're originally issued but not yet matured.

If interest rates have risen since the bond was issued, the bond is worth less and sells on the secondary market at a *discount*. For example, a $1,000 bond paying interest at 5 percent (called the *coupon rate*) when interest rates are 6 percent may actually sell for $900 — a $100 discount.

If interest rates have gone down, the bond sells at a *premium*. It's worth more because it pays higher-than-market interest.

The *yield* for a bond is the return you actually receive on your investment based on what you paid for it and the coupon interest rate. Yield is calculated by dividing the amount of annual interest by the bond purchase price. For example, if you purchase an 8 percent bond for $1,000, your yield is 8 percent ($80 divided by $1,000). If you buy the bond for $900, the yield is 8.89 percent. The higher the yield, the better your investment. (Of course, you also need to take into account the bond's rating as discussed earlier in this chapter.)

The Bonds Online Web site at www.bonds-online.com displays the yield, coupon rate, maturity, and other important characteristics for a list of bonds that meet your search criteria, as shown in Figure 5-1.

Figure 5-1: Bonds Online displays both major credit ratings, yield, price, and maturity for a list of bonds.

Moody's rating

S&P rating   Bond issuer

Corporate Query Results

Bonds Found: 228   Bonds Displayed: 1 through 100

Mdy	S&P	Qty	Min	Issue	Cpn	Maturity	Yld	LY	Price
A1	A+	30		Alabama Pw	6.000	03-01-2000	4.807	NC	100.210
A3	A-	72		Public Svc	6.000	05-01-2000	5.454	NC	100.176
Aa2	AA-	5		Kentucky U	5.950	06-15-2000	6.478	NC	99.750
Aaa	-	23		Chattanoog	0.000	07-01-2000	5.704	NC	97.090
Baa3	BBB-	100		Connecticu	5.750	07-01-2000C	5.746		100.000
A2	A	85		Southern C	5.875	01-15-2001	6.129	NC	99.737
Ba3	BB	5		Cms Energy	6.375	05-15-2001	8.061	NC	97.779
Aa3	AA-	25		Duke Energ	5.875	06-01-2001	6.460	NC	99.202
A2	A	50		Southern C	6.500	06-01-2001	6.561	NC	99.911
A3	A-	40		Virginia E	6.300	06-21-2001	6.567	NC	99.623
Baa2	BBB+	100		Niagara Mo	9.250	10-01-2001	6.913	NC	103.822
Baa1	A	36		Philadelph	5.625	11-01-2001	6.913	NC	97.778
Aaa	AAA	5		Public Svc	7.875	11-01-2001	5.923	NC	103.375
A3	A-	35		Public Svc	7.875	11-01-2001	6.490	NC	102.375
Ba3	BB	5		Cms Energy	7.125	11-15-2001C	8.133	MAT	98.232

Understanding Bond Variations and Features

Although bonds have a nice-girl reputation as low-risk investments, many types of bonds are as risky as any stock. Thousands of variations are out there. Many brokers make their living speculating and trading in bonds based on these variations and the ever-fluctuating interest rates.

A checklist of bond features

Here are a few of the different bond features you can find by perusing the Web:

■ **The credit rating of the entity issuing the bond:** This rating reflects the likelihood that the issuer will default on the bond.

■ **Coupon rate:** The rate of interest that the bond pays.

■ **When interest is paid:** The interest may be paid quarterly, semi-annually, annually, or upon maturity.

■ **Maturity date:** This refers to the date when you get back your original investment plus any unpaid interest.

■ **Whether the bond is indexed for inflation:** If the bond is indexed in this way, the bond pays an amount above the interest to compensate for inflation.

■ **Premiums and discounts:** These amounts reflect the value of bonds on the secondary market due to fluctuating interest rates.

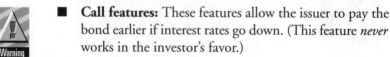

■ **Call features:** These features allow the issuer to pay the bond earlier if interest rates go down. (This feature *never* works in the investor's favor.)

Differentiating notes and bills

Often when investors and Web sites talk about bonds, they're referring to instruments technically and correctly called *notes* and *bills*. You'll see these terms on the Web, and knowing what they mean is important.

Bonds, notes, and bills are called *fixed-income securities* because the amount of income you earn is predetermined. Whether a fixed-income security is a bond, note, or bill depends solely upon its maturity date. The distinctions are as follows:

- **Bonds:** The maturity date is more than ten years from the issue date.

- **Notes:** The maturity date is between one and ten years from the date of issue.

- **Bills:** The maturity date is within one year from the issue date.

Finding bond funds on the Web

Bond funds provide you with additional diversification in your bond portfolio. Experts carefully balance risks, yields, and tax benefits to come up with a bond mix to attract investors.

Unfortunately, at the time of this printing, no Web sites are devoted to evaluating and comparing bond funds. You need to contact individual brokerages through their Web sites and find out what they offer in the way of bond funds.

Researching tax advantages of bonds

Certain bonds offer great income tax benefits. State and municipal bonds are popular because the interest earned isn't subject to federal income tax. And better yet, U.S. government bonds aren't subject to state and local taxes. You can locate and purchase a complete array of tax-free bonds at the BondAgent.com Web site located at `www.taxfreebond.com`.

Researching Bond Basics Online

Bond research on the Web can be a real eye-opener. If you've always thought of bonds as a simple IOU, you may be surprised to see a lot of bond Web sites geared toward bond brokers and speculators. In fact, finding a Web site that's geared toward the needs of an individual online investor may take some surfing.

The Bond Market Association is a not-for-profit organization made up of about 265 institutional members — bond issuers and investment groups. The Web site, located at www.investinginbonds.com, offers checklists and other materials to bond investors free of charge:

Figure 5-2: Web site of the Bond Market Association.

The Motley Fool Web site at www.fool.com is maintained by a couple of highly successful laughing-all-the-way-to-the-bank investment advisors. You unfortunately run into tons of paid advertising on the Motley Fool site, including lots of advertisements that hawk the Motley Fool investment books for sale at Amazon.com.

Aside from the commercial offerings, however, you can also find excellent explanations of bond basics that are anything but foolish. To get to the bond material, start at the Motley Fool home page and click Fool's School ☞ Investing Basics ☞ Bonds.

Visiting the U.S. Treasury Web Site

U.S. government bonds are considered one of the safest investments in the world. You can research, evaluate, and purchase such bonds using the free services on the U.S. Public Debt Web site located at `www.publicdebt.treas.gov`, as shown in Figure 5-3.

Congress sets limits on the total dollar value of securities that the Treasury can have outstanding at one time. From time to time, however, Congress increases the public debt limit. You can find out about new issues of Treasuries, read about the types offered, and buy them online on the Public Debt Web site.

Figure 5-3:   The U.S. Treasury home page.

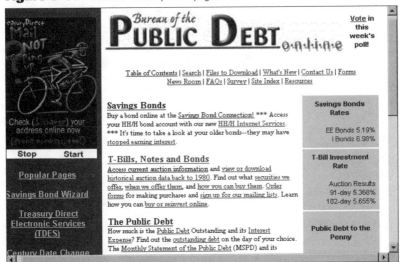

Finding Treasuries on the Web

After you decide to buy Treasuries, your research is far from over. The U.S. government offers you lots of choices. You can select from the following:

U.S. bonds, notes, and bills are called *Treasuries* because they're sold by the Treasury Department through its sub-agency, the Bureau of Public Debt.

- **Treasury bills (T-bills):** T-bills are short-term bonds with maturities of 13 weeks, 26 weeks, and 52 weeks. The Treasury periodically holds an *auction* in which it posts notices of new issues and makes them available to the public on the Web. The 52-week T-bills pay interest semiannually, and the 13- and 26-week varieties pay interest when they mature. T-bills come in minimum denominations of $1,000.

- **Treasury zero coupon bonds:** These bonds earn interest to reach their stated face value upon maturity. For example, you may purchase a $10,000 bond for $5,000. They're a favorite for college savings. Because these bonds don't pay interest until you cash them in, you don't have to report the interest as income before you redeem them.

- **Treasury notes:** This type of bond has a maturity date of two years, five years, or ten years. You're paid interest semi-annually and have to invest at least $1,000.

- **Treasury bonds:** This type of bond represents the government's longest-term bonds, having a 30-year maturity date. The Treasury sells them three times a year in multiples of $1,000. They pay interest semiannually.

- **Inflation-indexed notes:** These bonds are the new kids on the auction block — they were first introduced in January 1997. They pay a fixed rate of interest *plus* an extra amount to reflect the current inflation rate. The inflation adjustment is based on the consumer price index. These notes pay interest semiannually, have a ten-year maturity date, and are auctioned every three months.

Buying Treasuries online

The U.S. government is competing for your investment dollars. In an effort to make buying its bonds more convenient for you, the government offers you some pretty good customer service on the Web via its TreasuryDirect program.

The TreasuryDirect program allows you to buy bonds online directly from the government, completely avoiding a brokerage firm. A single TreasuryDirect account holds all of your notes, bills, and bonds.

You can open a TreasuryDirect account online and start purchasing bonds within minutes. Then you can do all of your account transactions online using the TreasuryDirect Virtual Lobby Web page shown in Figure 5-4.

Figure 5-4:   The TreasuryDirect Virtual Lobby.

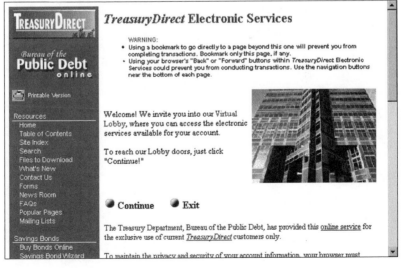

Using other Treasury online services

The Public Debt Web site is truly an example of government working for you. In addition to simplifying the process of researching and buying Treasuries, the site provides the following information and services at the www.publicdebt.treas.gov Web site (click the <u>Savings Bonds</u> hyperlink):

- **Lists of frequently asked questions:** You can click the <u>FAQs</u> link to learn more about bonds, notes, and bills.

- **Prevailing interest rates:** The Web site provides you with information as to the rate of interest currently being paid on bonds, notes, and T-bills, and the current costs of the various instruments.

- **Auction information:** The Bureau of Public Debt posts auction date schedules for new issues of T-bills and inflation-indexed notes.

- **Fun calculators:** These are free software programs that you can use to figure investment growth, tax advantages, and long-term savings goals.

CHAPTER 6

OPENING AN ONLINE BROKERAGE ACCOUNT

IN THIS CHAPTER

- Understanding what online brokers do
- Assessing your service needs
- Comparing commissions, costs, and services
- Opening an online brokerage account

In this chapter, I assume that you're not interested in paying full-service commissions to a full-service broker — that you want to pretty much keep things between you and your computer.

But no man (or woman) is an island — even one with a really fast modem. Although you've decided to replace your personal broker with a PC, you still need to establish an online brokerage account to buy and sell investments on the Web. With more than a hundred discount brokers online and vying for your account business, you shouldn't have too much trouble. This chapter tells you how to find one that delivers what you need.

Looking over Online Brokerage Services

You can purchase most things these days by entering your credit card number on a Web site. But you can't buy everything this way. To trade stocks, bonds, mutual fund shares, or other securities, you must first open an online brokerage account through a brokerage firm.

In the world of Web-based trading, your online brokerage firm is responsible for

- **Executing trades:** When you tell a brokerage firm that you want to buy or sell stocks, bonds, mutual fund shares, or other securities, the firm is responsible for communicating with the *securities exchange* or entity through which these securities are sold.

- **Maintaining account records:** The brokerage firm is responsible for maintaining information about the assets held in your account and updating this information periodically.

- **Providing updates and information:** Your online brokerage firm is an important link to the investing world. The firm's Web site should provide quotes, updates of the market, and access to charts, news, and research reports.

- **Providing other convenient services:** You may get the benefit of free checking and other handy services with a particular broker.

Finding a Reputable Online Broker

How do you find a broker that's reputable? Protecting yourself isn't difficult, but traps for the unwary are still out there. For starters, be sure to choose a broker that meets the following criteria:

- **SIPC insured:** The Securities Investor Protection Corporation (SIPC) currently insures securities and cash in a brokerage account for up to $500,000 (but no more than $100,000 of that may be in cash).

- **Listed on survey sites:** Select a broker that is evaluated on the Gomez Advisors and SmartMoney Web sites (which I discuss later in this chapter) or at least gets a good write-up in a national magazine. Stay away from brokerage firms that haven't been prescreened on these sites or by the media.

- **Look for objective referrals:** Steer clear of chat room advice from unknown sources whose motives and credentials you can't discern. (As a matter of fact, you can't even tell when chat room information was last updated.) Your goal is to avoid online sales pitches disguised as "hot tips."

Understanding Commissions, Costs, and Fees

Looking for a broker with low commissions? You should always try to get the most for your money, but a broker's advertised commissions may not tell the whole story.

Questioning the advertised commission

Sometimes you'll see a broker advertise a "flat-rate" commission or "commissions starting at" a certain amount.

You need to make sure when you're comparing commissions that you're comparing apples to apples. Make sure that you ask whether advertised commissions change based on the following:

- **The type of order placed:** Commissions may vary depending on whether you're placing a market or a limit order. A *market order* directs your broker to buy or sell shares at the best market price currently available. A *limit order* directs the broker to buy or sell shares only at a specified maximum or minimum price. Brokers may charge a higher commission for executing a limit order, but only advertise the lower fee they charge for a market order. Be sure to check. (I discuss market and limit orders in Chapter 7.)

■ **The kind of securities you're buying:** Sometimes brokers charge a higher commission for buying or selling an over-the-counter stock as opposed to a listed stock. A *listed stock* is one that is traded on a major stock exchange — such as the American Stock Exchange or the New York Stock Exchange. A stock that isn't listed is called an *over-the-counter stock*. NASDAQ is the leading market for over-the-counter stocks. (Most investors afford NASDAQ stocks the same status and prestige as stocks listed on exchanges.)

■ **How many shares you're buying or selling at one time:** An advertised "flat-rate" commission may be good only up to a certain number of shares. Find out how many shares you can buy or sell before a surcharge applies to the flat rate.

Looking for hidden fees and costs

You may think that commissions are the only costs involved with online trading. Unfortunately, this isn't the case. Several types of hidden costs can nibble away at your investment profits.

Here are a few fees to watch for, when opening an account, all considerations being equal:

■ **Fees to close the account:** Some brokerages charge a fee of $50 or more to close an active account.

■ **Charges for a copy of your statement:** If you need a copy of a prior month's statement that isn't online or simply would like to receive your statements in the mail, you can be charged up to $10 per page.

■ **Charges for transferring funds to or from your account:** If you need access to the funds in your account or plan to purchase additional securities by wiring funds, you should inquire about any associated charges for these types of transactions.

Asking the Right Questions before Deciding on a Brokerage

Online brokerage services are competitive and eager for your business. They offer an ever-increasing and innovative range of services to entice you to open an account with them. Accordingly, use the following checklist to determine which services interest you, and remember to ask who offers them:

- **Do quoted commission costs vary?** Does the advertised low commission vary with the size of the trade? Is there a minimum charge for small trades? A surcharge for a maximum number of shares?

- **Are there other transaction costs?** Does any "handling" or "service fee" or other transaction charge apply in addition to the commission?

- **Are minimum deposits and balances required?** What is the minimum required initial deposit? Am I required to maintain a minimum balance in the account?

- **What types of orders are accepted?** Does the online brokerage accept the types of orders you may want to make? What is the policy for cancelled orders?

- **How quickly are orders filled?** Does the brokerage have the ability to quickly execute orders so that you can take advantage of changes in the market throughout the day?

- **How quickly are orders confirmed?** Does the online brokerage service give you immediate confirmation that an order has been executed?

- **What emergency communications are available?** Can you reach the broker by fax or by telephone in case you can't get online or get to a computer?

- **What portfolio information do you receive?** How often is your account information updated? Will you receive an income tax summary? A transaction summary?

■ **Does the firm pay interest on idle funds?** If you maintain a substantial cash balance in the account, does the brokerage firm pay interest on "idle" funds? Some brokerage accounts automatically "sweep" idle funds to a higher-interest-bearing account.

■ **What research resources are available?** Does your brokerage make reports and research available to you? If so, is this service subject to an additional charge?

■ **What checking and wiring services are available?** Do you receive free checking services? Can you wire funds to and from the account free of charge?

■ **How is the brokerage firm rated by the experts?** How do the services of the brokerage firm measure up using the online rating services I discuss later in this chapter?

■ **Do you get price quote information?** Some online brokerage services, such as Datek, offer continuous price quote information. The Datek Online Web site, shown in Figure 6-1, offers a continuous price quote service called *data streaming*.

Figure 6-1:   Some brokerages offer current price quotes.

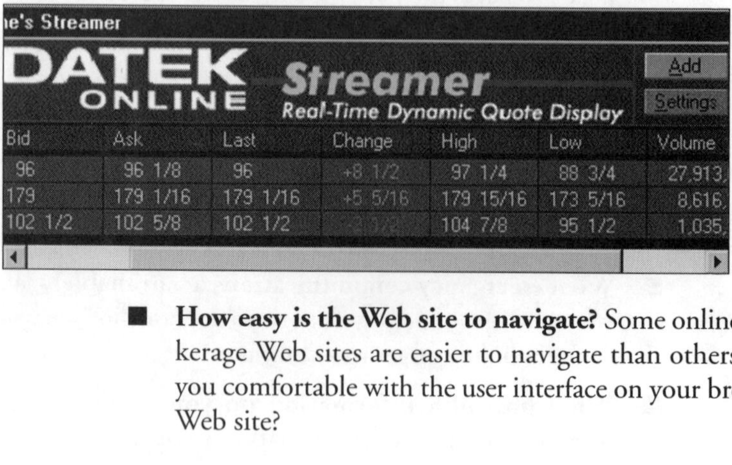

■ **How easy is the Web site to navigate?** Some online brokerage Web sites are easier to navigate than others. Are you comfortable with the user interface on your broker's Web site?

■ **How easy is it to connect to the Web site?** The Smart-Money Web site, which I discuss later in this chapter, offers a Broker Meter that tells you how long it takes to connect to particular broker's Web site.

■ **Do you get portfolio tracking and alerts?** Does your online brokerage provide portfolio tracking services such as online software? Does the brokerage provide services to alert you to important changes in your portfolio?

■ **Can you trade bonds, foreign securities, and derivatives?** Not all brokers trade bonds, foreign securities, and derivatives such as options. If *you* trade them, then you want to make sure your online brokerage does, too.

■ **How's the customer support?** How do the Gomez and SmartMoney Web sites, which I discuss in the next section, rate the brokerage's customer support? Can you access it by phone? By fax? Do you have to hold forever when you call?

Online Brokerage Rating Services

With more than a hundred brokers online, narrowing the field to come up with a short list is a good idea. Then you can ask each finalist the specific questions I provide in the checklist in the previous section. To help you come up with your short list, I critique several Web sites devoted to rating, ranking and critiquing online brokers in this section.

The Gomez ranking services

Gomez Advisors is an independent consulting firm that rates brokers several times a year. The Gomez site is the oldest, most authoritative, and most respected Web site for this purpose. You can find no better place to start in your screening efforts.

Figure 6-2: Gomez ranks the top 20 online brokerages.

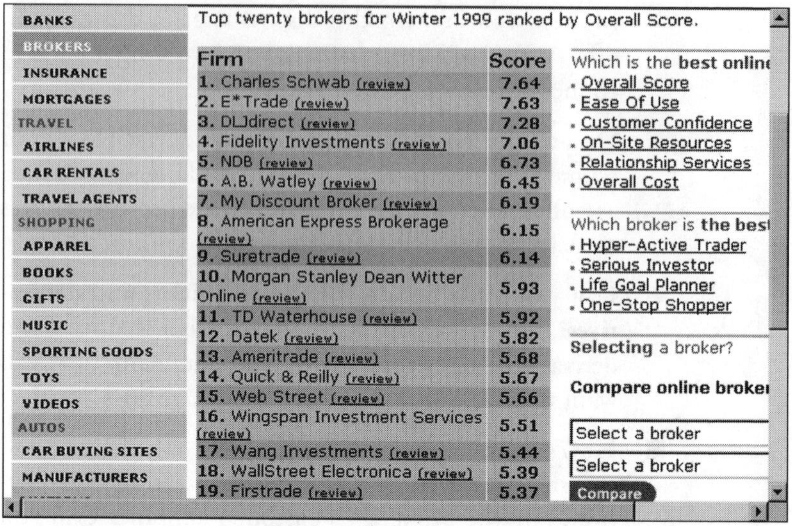

You can access the Gomez broker ratings at www.gomez.com by clicking the <u>Brokers</u> hyperlink. You can screen brokerage firms by using over a dozen different criteria and applying several different ranking systems. To view a list of the top 20 brokers, as shown in Figure 6-2, click the <u>Overall</u> hyperlink. The Overall ranking takes into account the following measurements:

- **Ease of use:** This measurement evaluates whether the account has demos, tutorials, well-integrated features, and customizing capability.

- **Customer confidence/relationship services:** This measurement tells you how well the customers like the Web site, based on their survey responses.

- **On-site resources:** This measurement indicates whether you can view recommendations and advisory reports on the site.

- **Overall cost:** This measurement compares commissions and transaction fees.

Figure 6-3:   Research a specific firm's ratings.

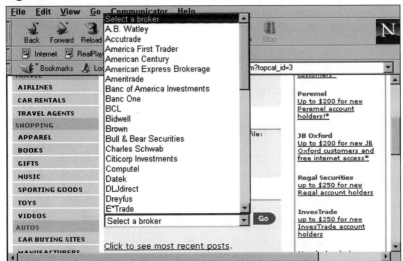

You can also click a link for each of the specific criteria above to see how brokerages fared in a particular area.

Gomez also allows you to research a specific online brokerage firm by name. You can enter the brokerage name by using the drop-down list on the home page, as shown in Figure 6-3. You can then see how the particular firm you've selected fares in the various Gomez ranking categories.

You can even search for a broker that complements your specific trading habits. For example, Gomez offers you links for brokers who cater to each of the following:

- **The hyperactive trader:** Services for this type of trader include online brokerage services offering low-cost trading, a simple interface, and fast execution.

- **The serious investor:** These services emphasize online brokerages that offer high-quality information tools and research.

■ **The life goal planner:** This area identifies brokerages that help locate mutual funds emphasizing long-term growth.

■ **The one-stop shopper:** These services include brokers that cater to the investor who wants to be able to trade a full range of securities on a single Web site.

Visiting the SmartMoney site

The SmartMoney Web site is a lot of fun to read. This is a great place to go for a second opinion after checking the more comprehensive Gomez Advisors site.

Like the Gomez Advisors site, the SmartMoney Web site (www.smartmoney.com) ranks brokers using an overall composite score and also ranks them in individual categories. Access these rankings by clicking Tools ☞ Broker Meter ☞ Broker Ratings. You can view the specific grading criteria by clicking the Extra Services, Responsiveness, and Reliability hyperlinks, as shown in Figure 6-4.

Figure 6-4: SmartMoney links to various brokerage rankings.

(c) 2000 SmartMoney.com

Besides offering entertaining narrative, the site has a few other unique features. For example, it identifies the *worst* brokerages in each category — some surprisingly large companies. It also offers a feature called the Broker Meter, which reports on how long it takes to access a broker's Web site.

Narrative reports on brokerage firms

Another good source of information is the monthly Discount Stockbrokers Ranked report by Sonic Net, located at `www.sonic.net/donaldj`. This Web site reviews about 80 brokers a month and compares them based on commissions and services.

Like the SmartMoney site, Sonic Net provides reviews of brokers in an easy-to-read narrative format. The site describes consumer experiences with the brokerages and provides a scathing report on "problem" brokers each month.

Opening Your Account: The Process

Opening an account varies a bit from brokerage firm to brokerage firm. But the basic process is the same. You must first access the Web site for the brokerage firm. You then find a link that says something like <u>open an account now</u> (this link is unsurprisingly easy to locate) and perform some variation of the following steps:

1. Complete a secure online application. The application asks you questions like your Social Security number, whether you're opening a joint account, and other information necessary to get you set up on the company's system.

2. Return your signed application by mail. Some firms allow you to receive an account number and begin trading right away, but your signed application must be received within three days of your first trade.

3. Fund your account. You can get money into your account by mailing a check, providing a credit card number, or authorizing the brokerage to create an electronic check from an existing account, depending on the policies of the brokerage.

Should you open more than one brokerage account? On one hand, you want to avoid opening more accounts than you need, because this tactic can increase fees. On the other hand, the Gomez Advisors recommend that you consider opening a second account with a smaller, less-heavily-trafficked brokerage firm if your primary account is with a popular firm that may experience periodic capacity overloads and transaction delays.

Bypassing the Broker with a DRIP Account

You can skip the broker altogether by purchasing stock from a company that offers a *Dividend Reinvestment Plan*. Over 800 publicly traded companies offer Dividend Reinvestment Plans, called DRIPs. These companies allow shareholders to invest in a special program where dividends are constantly reinvested to purchase more stocks.

You can find out more about DRIPs by visiting the DRIP Central Web site, located at www.dripcentral.com and shown in Figure 6-5. Click the drip investing guide link for a tour of the basics or the drip services link for a complete list of companies that offer DRIPs.

Figure 6-5:   The DRIP Central Web site.

CHAPTER 7
MAKING YOUR FIRST ONLINE TRADE

IN THIS CHAPTER

- Getting a current quote

- Placing different types of orders

- Canceling an order

- Executing and confirming a trade

- Trading when the markets are closed

- Coping with the times that you can't get online

When you decide that a stock is selling at the right price — or is about to be — it's time to move quickly. This chapter tells you how to place an order and explains how you decide what *type* of order to place. (In fact, you can initiate four different types of orders.)

Getting the Current Market Price

You can't be an informed buyer or seller if you don't know the most basic information — the price. Stock prices can change in a matter of seconds. Mutual funds shares are revalued daily. Bonds sold on the secondary market are less volatile, but can also change value quickly. Before you take the plunge, you need some relatively current price data.

Your online brokerage's Web site is likely to provide current market quotes. If not, you can get them for free at plenty of other Web sites. For example, the CNBC Web site at www.cnbc.com shown in Figure 7-1 provides daily price data for stocks, bonds, and mutual funds. It's a free service, supported entirely by advertising.

Other services, such as Datek Online, provide continuous real-time quotes (as opposed to quotes subject to the usual 15-minute delay). I discuss Datek's streaming service in Chapter 1.

Figure 7-1:   Web sites such as this one provide free stock quotes.

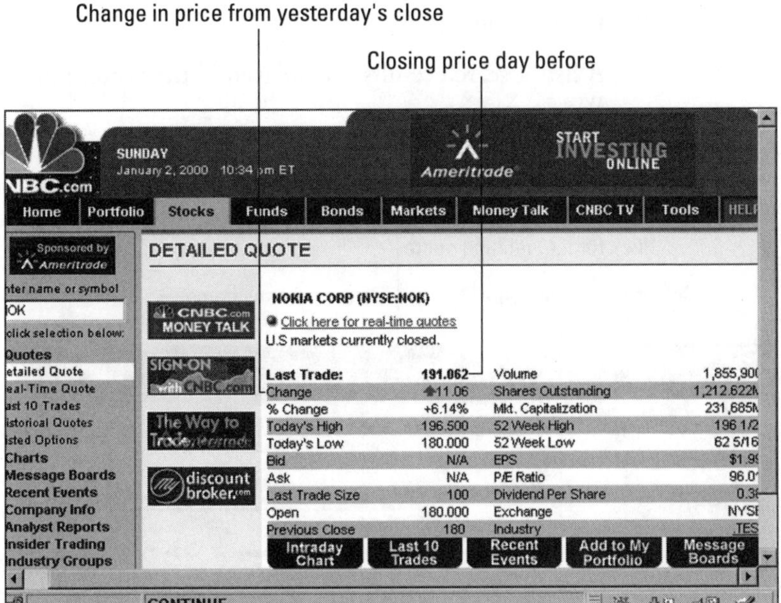

Change in price from yesterday's close

Closing price day before

Stock quote formats differ greatly from site to site. However, they all show the stock on close of the last trading day and the *net change* since closing. The net change is the increase or decrease in price since the close of trading on the previous day. You then figure the current price by adding or subtracting the net change. The current price of the Nokia stock, according to the information in Figure 7-1, is $202.122 ($191.062 + $11.06).

To get stock, bond, or mutual fund pricing information, you must first know the company's abbreviation, or ticker symbol. You can find it using the CNBC Symbol Lookup service at www.cnbc.com. To search for a ticker symbol on the CNBC Web site:

1. Select the investment type, as shown in Figure 7-2.

2. Enter the company name in the blank field.

3. Click Submit.

A list of search results is displayed at the bottom of the Web page.

Figure 7-2: Searching for the Nokia Corporation ticker symbol.

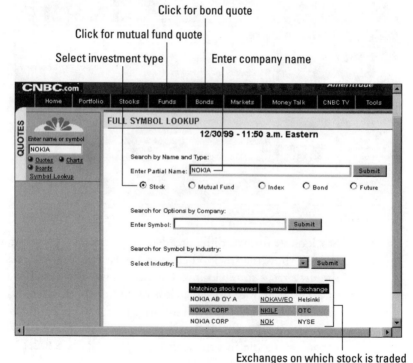

Click for bond quote

Click for mutual fund quote

Select investment type

Enter company name

Exchanges on which stock is traded

Figure 7-2 shows a search for stock of the Nokia Corporation, for which the ticker symbol is NOK. The search results also display the exchanges on which the stock is traded and the full company name.

Deciding What Kind of Order to Place

Trading a stock requires more than merely picking a company and monitoring its price. Your decisions concerning the conditions under which you place the order can also mean a great deal of money to you. For example, do you want to buy the stock at the current market price (whatever that may be), or do you want to only buy the stock if it reaches a particular price?

You can choose from four types of orders: market, limit, stop, and stop limit. Most online brokerage Web sites allow you to specify the type of trade by using a drop-down menu, such as the one shown for Datek Online in Figure 7-3. Understanding the implications of each type of trade is important to successful online investing; the following sections explain each order type.

Figure 7-3:   Select the type of order you want to place from your brokerage's Web site.

Buying at market

When you place a *market order,* you're directing the brokerage to buy or sell a specified quantity of stock at the current market price. Because the price of a stock changes constantly, you may find yourself placing an order when the stock is at one price, only to find that it's filled at a different price. The price may have moved an eighth of a point or more in the intervening minutes.

A market order automatically expires at the end of the trading day. If you place an order after the close of trading (for example, late at night), it's technically good for the entire next trading day. In practice, it's usually filled immediately after the opening of trading.

The advantage of market orders is that they can always be filled, because you're willing to pay the prevailing price. The disadvantage is that when volatile markets are on the move, you may get sticker shock.

Market orders are the most popular type of order. In most cases, a market order serves your purposes.

Issuing a limit order

Limit orders provide you with the convenience of not having to constantly watch the market. They can also protect you against dramatic movements in the market.

A *limit order* directs the brokerage to buy or sell stock when the price drops or rises to a specific number. When you place a limit order, the brokerage is limited to

- ■ Buying the stock at the specified price or lower.
- ■ Selling the stock at the specified price or higher.

For example, a limit order to purchase 500 shares of XYZ stock at $40.00 a share means the broker may fill the order at $40.00 or less, but not at $$^{40}\!/_{18}$ per share. Alternatively, a limit order to sell at $40.00 means that the broker can't accept a fraction of a penny less than $40.00 for your stock.

When you place a limit order, you need to specify whether the order is a day order or a good till canceled (GTC) order. A *day order* expires at the end of the trading day. A *GTC order* doesn't expire. You have to remember to cancel it, as I discuss later in this chapter.

Placing a stop order

A *stop order* is a contingency order that becomes a market order when the stock trades, is bid, or is offered at a specific price. Stop orders differ from limit orders because stop orders happen at a particular price rather than within a price range like a limit order.

A stop order can help you stay in control of your portfolio during a period of time when you can't get to your computer or reach your broker by phone. Stop orders are also very helpful when the market is on the move.

For example, if you purchased XYZ stock at $45.00 a share hoping it would go up, but now the price is dropping, you may want to limit your losses by placing a stop order to sell the stock if the price drops to $42.00 a share.

Understanding the complex stop limit order

A *stop limit order* is a contingency order that becomes a limit order when the security trades, is bid, or is offered at a specific price. It helps you take advantage of sudden movement in the market while limiting your risk. It's more complicated to understand than the other types of orders, but can be very useful to you given the right market conditions.

An example of a stop limit order is "Buy 100 shares of XYZ stock; stop at $120.00 with a limit of $120¼." This means you want your order to be activated to purchase stock at

$120.00 per share, but not if it goes above $120¼ per share. Sell stops are used below the market price, and buy stops are used above the market price.

The advantage of this type of order is that it gives you more control over the price at which your order is filled. The disadvantage is that your order may go unfilled if your specifications can't be met.

Another variation: Fill or kill

The so-called *fill or kill* instruction has a name that's pretty descriptive of its function. Some online brokerage services allow you to specify that a limit order should expire — or be killed — if it can't be executed within a certain time frame.

Executing, Confirming, and Canceling Orders

Are you ready to invest a chunk of your savings with a couple clicks of your mouse? Indeed, all it takes is a few clicks to reallocate or change the character of your portfolio.

Executing and confirming an order

Now that you've scoped out the market, you're ready to make a move. Fortunately, it's easy to act with most online brokerages, barring the occasional technological glitch.

The procedure for executing a trade is pretty similar from brokerage to brokerage, but the user interface that appears on your screen varies. The Web page for entering orders with the Datek Online brokerage is shown in Figure 7-4.

Figure 7-4: The Datek Web site makes it easy to place trade orders.

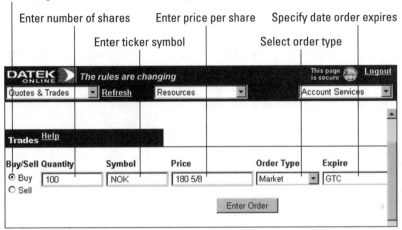

Regardless of which online brokerage you use to place a trade, you need to have the following information ready to enter:

- **Quantity:** Specify the number of shares of stock you want to buy or sell.

- **Ticker symbol:** You must enter the ticker symbol for the stock you want to trade.

- **Price:** Enter the price at which you want to buy or sell the stock.

- **Order type:** Indicate whether you want to place a market, limit, stop, or other type of order.

- **Expiration:** Specify when you want the order to expire.

After you place your order, a confirmation message appears on your screen. If this message doesn't appear, call the brokerage immediately. If you simply repeat the steps you took to enter the trade, you may end up owning *twice* as much stock as you planned.

Canceling or changing an order

Changed your mind? Got cold feet? Fortunately, canceling or changing an order online is *not* a complicated proposition.

All brokerages allow you to cancel an order before the brokerage executes the trade — but most charge a fee. Normally, canceling an order costs $10.00 or less, and you accomplish it pretty much the same way you placed your initial order.

Canceling an order usually takes about as much time as placing one. Unfortunately, scrapping your order can seem painfully slow in a volatile market when you've changed your mind. Don't be surprised if your cancellation is confirmed moments *after* your order is filled (and once your order is executed, you can't turn back). It's nobody's fault; that's everyday life in the world of online investing.

Taking Advantage of After-Hours Trading

After-hours trading when the NYSE and NASDAQ are closed is the newest rage. It's made possible by the emergence of the ECN. When you use an ECN to trade after hours, you're trading exclusively with other investors using that ECN. The ECN uses an electronic order-matching system that automatically pairs up limit orders to buy and sell.

Trading after hours has definite advantages — you have more time at night, and it's quieter because the kids are asleep. But it can also present some unique risks.

The Datek Online Web site warns its customers to be wary of the following issues:

■ You may encounter wider *spreads* between bids and offers than during usual market hours. This difference means that the ECN gets to pocket a larger portion of the price you pay or receive for stock.

■ You're competing against professional traders with more information and analysis.

■ Some stocks are very *liquid* (they sell quickly) during extended-hours sessions; others aren't liquid at all (nobody wants to buy them). This situation happens because you're limited to trading with other ECN users during after-hours sessions.

■ News stories may have a greater impact on stock prices, and in general, stock prices may be more volatile.

When you trade on the ECN, special trading rules may apply. At a minimum, expect to encounter the following restrictions:

■ Only NASDAQ stocks are available for trading during after-hours sessions. NYSE and American Stock Exchange securities are not eligible for extended-hours trading.

■ ECNs usually accept only limit orders for participation during after-hours trading sessions. Market orders and stop orders aren't accepted at these times.

Coping When You Can't Connect

It's bound to happen. Perhaps a problem occurs with your broker's Web site or a local ISP server, or maybe it's the telephone lines. But for whatever reason, you can't connect to your broker.

Here are a few precautionary and coping strategies:

■ **Use an online brokerage that offers telephone trading as well as online services:** This feature can be difficult to find, because fewer online brokerages than you may think offer you the option of placing a trade by phone. Don't assume that yours does — ask.

■ **Open more than one online brokerage account:** If traffic is heavy on one brokerage site, maybe you can place your trade on another site experiencing less volume.

■ **Enter trades of less than 1,000 shares on the NAS-DAQ:** The NASDAQ offers some safeguards that are an outgrowth of the 1987 stock market crash, when market makers' phones went unanswered as stocks plummeted. A current regulation — called *SOES* — requires that trades of less than 1,000 shares on the NASDAQ must be swiftly executed. SOES stands for *Small Order Execution System*, and it requires that trades of less than 1,000 shares be executed within a matter of minutes. When things get desperate, consider trading large amounts of stock in separate trades of less than 1,000 shares.

CHAPTER 8

MAINTAINING YOUR PORTFOLIO

IN THIS CHAPTER

- Deciding when to sell an investment
- Keeping track of the paperwork
- Tracking your portfolio online

Remember the tortoise and the hare? Some investments are hares; others are tortoises. Sometimes your hare stays the course and makes you a winner. Sometimes it's your safe, steady tortoise of an investment that meets the NAIC goal of doubling your investment in five years. Or maybe the hare and the tortoise both take a snooze.

This chapter tells you how to monitor and track the performance of your investments and how to decide when and if it's time to pull your bets from a lagging contender.

Deciding When to Sell a Stock

Even failed relationships are full of promise at the start. No one buys an investment expecting to sell it at a loss. But it happens.

If you're investing with long-term goals in mind, do you try to ride out the rough spots? Or is it wiser to sever yourself from an investment headed south? Both strategies have their time and place. And to complicate things further, experts sometimes advise selling a *profitable* investment if a better opportunity comes along.

Table 8-1 highlights seven scenarios that might induce an informed investor to consider selling a stock.

Table 8-1: When to Consider Selling a Stock

Scenario	Why to Consider Selling
You observe fundamental changes in market dynamics or management.	Events that spell uncertainty for the company or industry should cause you to reevaluate your investment.
Profits are both lagging and not satisfactorily explained.	Sometimes the company provides a good (and temporary) reason why profits don't meet expectations. But if you don't feel that the explanation is satisfactory, plausible, and encouraging, it may be time to sell.
The company's growth cycle has peaked.	New companies that fill a market niche can experience a meteoric rise in the early years. But profits peak and level off as competition increases. If recent growth has been stagnant for a previously profitable investment, it may be time to cash out and move on to new horizons.
You can use a tax loss in the current year.	If you can sell an investment at a loss in a year when you're facing high taxes, you may be wiser to write it off now than wait for a rebound.
The SSG shows substantial changes.	Completing a new Stock Selection Guide (SSG) form, as I discuss in Chapter 3, can help you pinpoint factors that may have changed since you first purchased the investment.
The critics pan it.	If several respected analysts and publications are suddenly giving an investment the thumbs down, you should at least consider their reasoning.
A better opportunity comes along.	Sometimes a good investment needs to be replaced with a better one to maximize the overall performance of your portfolio.

Rolling Over Your Mutual Funds

Usually, the best strategy for mutual funds is hands off! You want to avoid churning your mutual funds for a couple of good reasons:

■ **You generally have to pay a fee to get in or out of a mutual fund.** (I discuss load and redemption fees in Chapter 4.)

■ **You're paying for the management expertise of a fund manager who doubtless knows that the fund isn't performing well.** If you sell, then you may not benefit from the fund manager pruning the portfolio tree for non-performing stocks and cultivating better performance. Pulling out of the fund may cost you the benefit of the manager's rebounding strategy.

Nevertheless, at times you may see the writing on the wall that it's time to sell your fund shares. Table 8-2 outlines a few unfortunate scenarios that may rightfully cause you to lose faith.

Table 8-2: When to Consider Selling a Mutual Fund

Scenario	Why to Consider Selling
A change in fund management is followed by losses.	You need to keep up with changes in fund management and philosophy. If either of them no longer inspire your confidence based on performance, analyst reviews, or intuition, it's time to make a move.
An industry or sector on which the fund focuses is lagging.	Sometimes events that affect an industry or sector as a whole affect the future potential of your fund.
You've met your long-term goals.	After your investment has grown to a certain level, you may decide to invest some of your profits elsewhere and increase your level of diversification.

Deciding When to Part With a Bond

Because bonds mature all by themselves, the decision to end the investment relationship is made for you, to some extent, by the specified maturity date. But you may decide to sell a bond on the secondary market rather than wait for it to mature.

Bonds are less responsive to market rumors and hype than stocks. The value of a bond on the secondary market on any given day is determined by prevailing interest rates.

You may decide that a particular bond has no place in your portfolio if you experience any of the following scenarios:

Table 8-3: When to Consider Selling a Bond

Scenario	Why to Consider Selling
Interest rates are on the rise.	If you seriously suspect that you're headed for a period of high inflation and interest rates that may erode the real value of your investment, it may be time to sell.
You have more bonds than you need for diversification.	Bonds are important for stability and diversification, but if your portfolio consists of more than 40 percent bonds, you may consider selling off a few in favor of some higher-growth-oriented investments.
Events have affected the stability of your corporate bonds.	Corporate bonds are like stocks in that events that adversely impact the company may also affect the stability of your investment. A bond's credit rating can literally change overnight, and you need to keep current on changes that may affect the rating.

Saving the Right Paperwork

Did you think that as an online investor you'd be immune from a mailbox stuffed with investment paperwork? Not so. Your online investments are going to generate as much recycling fodder as your full-service brokerage ever did.

What must you save from the morning mail, and what can
you safely toss? This section gives you a few filing (and shred-
ding) tips.

Safekeeping the essential documents

Your online account begins generating paper before your first
trade. You even generate some of it yourself by downloading
and printing it from your computer. The following list highlights important documents that you want to save for your
records:

■ **The contract to open your online investing account:**
When you first open an online account, you're asked to
print out, sign, and mail an agreement. The instructions
for mailing a contract to open an account with Datek
Online are shown in Figure 8-1. The agreement contains
the current terms and conditions of your relationship
with the brokerage. You should save a downloaded copy
of the signed agreement in case the brokerage amends
the form in the future.

Figure 8-1:   Save a copy of your online brokerage agreement.

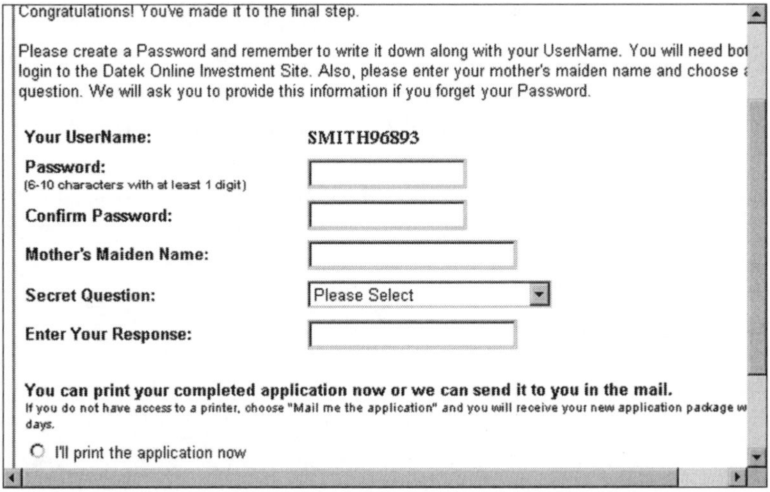

Congratulations! You've made it to the final step.

Please create a Password and remember to write it down along with your UserName. You will need bot
login to the Datek Online Investment Site. Also, please enter your mother's maiden name and choose ε
question. We will ask you to provide this information if you forget your Password.

Your UserName: SMITH96893

Password:
(6-10 characters with at least 1 digit)

Confirm Password:

Mother's Maiden Name:

Secret Question: Please Select

Enter Your Response:

You can print your completed application now or we can send it to you in the mail.
If you do not have access to a printer, choose "Mail me the application" and you will receive your new application package w
days.

○ I'll print the application now

■ **Account balance information:** When you access information about your account via the Web, you only get the current information. To maintain a history of your account activity, you need to print out hard copies of your account information or save it to a file every month.

■ **Brokerage statements:** Be sure to save the monthly or quarterly statements your brokerage sends you. You should save all these statements indefinitely, because the IRS may want to see your historical account information in the event of an audit.

■ **Annual summary:** You receive an annual summary from the brokerage that contains information to help you prepare your income taxes, but not as much detail about specific transactions as you get on the monthly and quarterly statements and trade confirmations. Hold onto the annual summaries for as long as you keep your account open or as long as you hold a certain investment.

■ **Form 1099:** Sometime after the close of the tax year but before January 31, you'll receive an IRS Form 1099 for each of your brokerage accounts. The 1099 discloses dividends, interest income, and capital gains distributions you received during the year. The IRS receives a copy of the 1099 and matches the information on its copy to what you report on your return. Save this form with your annual tax documents. A sample 1099 form is shown in Figure 8-2.

A good filing system is a must! A separate expanding file for each online account or investment you maintain works well.

Figure 8-2: Both the investor and the IRS get a copy of this form.

9191 ☐ VOID ☐ CORRECTED			

PAYER'S name, street address, city, state, ZIP code, and telephone no. | 1 Ordinary dividends $ | OMB No. 1545-0110 | **Dividends and Distributions**
| | 2a Total capital gain distr. $ | **2000** | |
| | | Form **1099-DIV** | |
PAYER'S Federal identification number | RECIPIENT'S identification number | 2b 28% rate gain $ | 2c Unrecap. sec. 1250 gain $ | **Copy A For Internal Revenue Service Center**
RECIPIENT'S name | | 2d Section 1202 gain $ | 3 Nontaxable distributions $ | File with Form 1096.
Street address (including apt. no.) | | 4 Federal income tax withheld $ | 5 Investment expenses $ | For Privacy Act and Paperwork Reduction Act
City, state, and ZIP code | | 6 Foreign tax paid $ | 7 Foreign country or U.S. possession | Notice, see the 2000 General Instructions for
Account number (optional) | 2nd TIN Not. ☐ | 8 Cash liquidation distr. $ | 9 Noncash liquidation distr. $ | Forms 1099, 1098, 5498, and W-2G.

Form **1099-DIV** Cat. No. 14415N Department of the Treasury - Internal Revenue Service

Do NOT Cut or Separate Forms on This Page — Do NOT Cut or Separate Forms on This Page

Discarding what you don't need

Luckily, not everything that you receive from your online brokerage has to be saved. Here are a few items you can safely toss:

- **Annual reports:** Annual reports take up a lot of space and contain tons of promotional hype, and the information you need is readily accessible elsewhere.

  If you want to do a comparison of a prior year's performance to that of the current year, you're better off getting your information from a source like *Value Line Investment Survey* or *Standard & Poor's Stock Guide*. These sources provide you with data for several prior years at a glance, already organized into a format that facilitates comparison. They're available for free at any public library.

- **Proxy notices:** A *proxy notice* informs you that, as a shareholder, you have a right to vote on pending matters such as the election of the board of directors. After the vote has been taken, you don't need to hang on to the proxy notice.

- **Advertisements:** You can pitch any advertising materials your brokerage sends you about stocks or investment opportunities as soon as you've reviewed them. Treat this information as you would any other unsolicited promotional mailings and give it the same shelf life.

■ **Individual transaction confirmations:** Save the individual transaction and trade confirmations that you get in the mail until you receive the monthly or quarterly statement that details each. Then you can safely discard these notifications.

Tracking Your Portfolio Online

Losing track of your existing portfolio while you're immersed in research of what to buy next is a mistake you can't afford to make. Keeping track of what you own and what it's worth is essential to your financial wellbeing.

Determining what to monitor

Before you decide on a portfolio tracking system, get a handle on what you want to monitor. You certainly don't want to waste a lot of time gathering extraneous information, nor can you afford to overlook critical data.

Most investment experts agree that, as a minimum, investors should keep tabs on the following:

■ What you own, how much of it you own, and its current value

■ What you may want to sell in the near future

■ What you may want to buy in the future — if the price moves into your range

You should also stay current with events that may affect a company or market sector in which you've invested. For example, a medical breakthrough that you see in the newspapers may cause you to reevaluate your health care-sector stocks.

Reevaluating investments is similar to your initial evaluation process. The Bloomberg Web site at `www.bloomberg.com` and the Morningstar Web site at `www.morningstar.com` are good sources of investment-related news that may spur you to look at your portfolio. See Chapters 4 and 6 for more information on these sites. Periodically reevaluating the vital signs of your investment by completing an updated Stock Selection Guide form (as I discuss in Chapter 3) is also a good idea.

Types of portfolio tracking software

Gone are the days when investors hovered over stock ticker machines, waiting to pick out the market price of each of their investments from a mass of endlessly curling tapes. Online portfolio tracking software lets you see changes to your investment values instantly and at a glance.

Today you can choose from among dozens of programs, which fall into three general categories:

- **Software that tracks current prices only:** Using this type of software, you enter the ticker symbol for each of your investments into a table. Every time you access the table, the program shows the current price of each of your stocks, updated automatically.

- **Programs that track historical data and current prices:** This type of system provides information about your purchase price, gains, losses, and recent trading activity as well as the current values. Because this type of system requires you to enter historical information, it can be time-consuming to set up initially.

- **Comprehensive asset tracking software:** Some software programs track all of the investments that comprise your net worth — not just securities. For example, you can use the portfolio tracking software available on the Quicken.com Web site to track the values of your home, cash accounts, and a variety of assets other than securities. To access the Quicken asset tracking software, point your browser to www.quicken.com and click the My Portfolio hyperlink.

Looking at Some Popular Portfolio Tracking Software

Most online brokerages offer portfolio tracking software, so see what yours has to offer. If you find it lacking with respect to any of your needs, consider checking out one or more of the popular programs discussed in this section.

Using the versatile Morningstar tracker

The Morningstar Web site (www.morningstar.com) allows you to create either a quick portfolio or a transaction portfolio, as shown in Figure 8-3.

■ **Quick portfolio:** This portfolio allows you to track the current price of your assets, which are displayed by their ticker symbols. Access this portfolio at the Morningstar Web site by clicking Home ☞ Portfolio ☞ Quick Portfolio.

■ **Transaction portfolio:** This portfolio displays historical data information as well as current price data. Seeing the historical information allows you to get a better handle on asset gains, losses, and trends. Access the transaction portfolio by clicking Home ☞ Portfolio ☞ Transaction Portfolio.

Figure 8-3: Morningstar offers two types of tracking software.

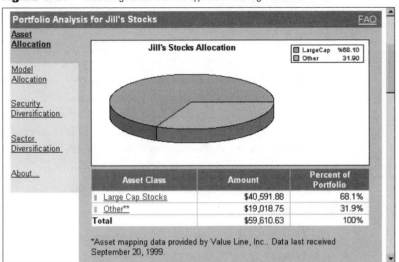

The comprehensive Yahoo! tracker

Sometimes you're after more than the current quotes. You can also use portfolio tracking software to help you analyze current trends and make decisions about your portfolio.

The Yahoo! portfolio tracker http://my.yahoo.com is a little more complicated to use than the Morningstar program, but it provides links to a wealth of information.

When you use the Yahoo! tracker to view ticker symbols and current price data, you can click links on the same screen to view the following:

■ Current news about the company

■ Recent analysts' reports and predictions about the investment

■ A company profile

■ Research tools and charts to help you analyze company data and trends

Viewing your portfolio graphically with Quicken

Access the portfolio tracker at the Quicken.com Web site (www.Quicken.com) by clicking the Portfolio hyperlink. The Quicken portfolio tracker allows you to view a graphical representation of your portfolio. A chart displays the allocation of assets of large-cap, small-cap, and international stocks, as well as bonds and money market funds. This tracker lets you actually *see* the extent to which you're diversified.

Tracking each transaction with Microsoft Investor

The Microsoft Investor portfolio tracking software allows you to enter each investment and recalculate your portfolio after every transaction. Access this invaluable service by navigating to www.investor.com and clicking the Portfolio link.

The downside of this particular tracker is that it's more difficult to install. Instead of simply going online to use it, you need to download a software plug-in to run the program on your system. After you've done so, though, you can even import transactions from Quicken or Microsoft Money for comprehensive tracking and analysis functions.

CHAPTER 9
AVOIDING ONLINE SCAMS

IN THIS CHAPTER

- Avoiding pump-and-dump schemes
- Watching out for stock scalping
- Recognizing bogus IPOs
- Finding Web sites that protect you

In the last year alone, the *New York Times* printed nearly 50 stories about Internet stock fraud and cyber-stock scams. No doubt the Web is a new communication medium for an old pastime: scamming people who are looking to get rich quick.

This chapter gives you pointers on how to protect yourself while investing on the Web. Your best defense is thorough and patient research.

Looking at Who Gets Cheated and How

How treacherous is the Internet? It's likely no more dangerous to the individual investor looking to get rich on a single hot tip than traditional investing has been. The increased potential for Internet cyber-scams lies in the Internet's ability to reach so many gullible investors in so short a time.

Most scams involve *penny stocks,* which are stocks that sell for less than a dollar per share. These stocks have a limited trading volume and a low share price, and these factors make it easier for the bad guys to significantly affect the price of the stock quickly. Effecting such a change in the price of heavily traded stocks listed on the New York Stock Exchange or the NASDAQ is much harder.

The pump and dump

The *pump-and-dump* scheme involves feeding false information onto the Web to pump up the price of a stock. The perpetrators of the scheme own a huge chunk of the company's stock prior to the scam, which they dump by selling it to eager investors who believe the rumors of an imminent takeover, scientific breakthrough, or whatever other story the unscrupulous promoters have concocted.

This scam was used to drive up the price of a technology company called Pairgain Technologies, Inc. The scammers posted a report to a Yahoo! message board claiming that an Israeli rival was buying out the Pairgain stock for a hefty price. The stock price quickly rose 30 percent as a result of the bogus report, which was cleverly disguised to look as if it had originated at the Bloomberg News site.

The stock closed at the end of the day as the 12th most heavily traded on the NASDAQ — ahead of even popular stocks like Amazon.com. After the rumor was exposed, however, share prices plummeted — leaving investors holding huge losses. Even sophisticated investors were taken in by the scam.

Verify the source of information that you act on. In the case of the bogus Pairgain Technologies stock, the report wasn't actually from Bloomberg News, but rather a clever forgery of the site. Check that the reports actually appear on the URLs that they say they do and that the URLs actually point to the Web site that they say they do.

Stock scalpers

Scalping is the practice of an "advisor" recommending that an investment group buy a particular stock that, unbeknownst to the group, the so-called advisor is trying to unload at a profit. The Federal Trade Commission has stepped up its efforts to prosecute such bogus stock tipsters.

An example of a scalping scheme was perpetrated by a man who went by the name of Tokyo Joe. A reputed financial guru, this man charged Web surfers up to $200 a month for his stock picks and other investment advice.

The Securities and Exchange Commission brought charges against Tokyo Joe and his company alleging that he misled his group into buying a stock that he had previously purchased and then sold at a profit to take advantage of the rise in price that his advice caused.

Tokyo Joe is hardly an isolated phenomenon. Hundreds of online investment newsletters offer stock picks and hot tips on the Web. SEC regulations require the newsletter writers to disclose who paid them in an effort to keep promotional material from being passed off as unbiased information. But government agencies often investigate only after someone gets burned and files a complaint.

Illegitimate IPOs

Yet another favorite of Internet scam artists is the irresistible *initial public offer*, or *IPO*. An IPO is an initial stock offering of a company that's being publicly traded for the first time. A legitimate IPO is considered a very attractive offering, because stock almost always increases in value, making a handsome profit for investors lucky enough to learn about an IPO. Similarly, the lure of a new venture promising big returns is just too much for some starry-eyed investors to resist.

You really have to be in the right place at the right time to hear about an IPO or a promising new business venture. You can get some reliable news and information about IPOs by visiting the Yahoo! Web site at www.yahoo.com and clicking <u>Reports</u> ☞ <u>IPO</u>. But the information is limited and often becomes available only after the initial offered shares have been purchased by those lucky enough to hear about it first.

Warning

Everyone wants to be the first to hear about an IPO. For this reason, bogus promoters of nonexistent IPOs and new venture companies promising big returns flourish on the Internet. Access the SEC Web site by navigating to www.sec.com; then click the <u>How to Avoid Internet Scams</u> hyperlink to see several examples of promoters who raised money for supposed IPOs and new business ventures over the Internet, but then pocketed the proceeds instead of capitalizing the company.

Web Sites That Protect You

You don't have to feel like helpless prey on the Web. Government regulatory agencies and consumer agencies are fighting crime and exposing scams with their own Web sites.

The following list provides a sampling of the Web sites working for you in this area:

■ **The NASD Regulation Web:** This site (www.nasdr.com), sponsored by the National Association of Securities Dealers, shown in Figure 9-1, provides a list of licensed brokers and previous disciplinary actions or complaints against them. You can also file a complaint of your own at this site.

Figure 9-1:   You can investigate a broker on the NASD site.

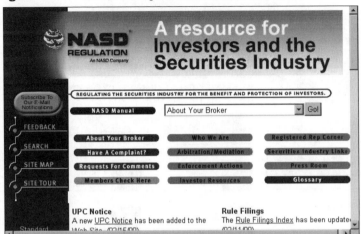

© 2000 NASD Regulation, Inc. (NASD Regulation). Reprinted with permission from NASD Regulation.

■ **The Federal Trade Commission:** This agency, which monitors securities activities, maintains a Web site at www.ftc.gov. Click Consumer Protection ☞ Investments to arrive at the Web page shown in Figure 9-2, which provides you with fraud alert information and extensive information on how to avoid getting burned online. You can also find out about the agency's latest regulatory efforts and interesting scams that the FTC has uncovered.

■ **The National Fraud Information Center:** This agency has its Web site at www.fraud.org and is dedicated to reporting and uncovering fraud on the Internet. It's a good place to go to check out an investment that sounds too good to be true. The National Consumers Organization, a well-respected, not-for-profit, consumer advocacy group, established and funds the site.

■ **The Stock Detective:** This commercial site, which you can find at www.stockdetective.com, is devoted to reporting all sorts of information about stocks, but with a special emphasis on reporting "stinky stocks" and cyber-scams.

Figure 9-2:   The FTC maintains its own Web site.

CLIFFSNOTES REVIEW

Use this CliffsNotes Review to practice what you learn in this book and to build your confidence in making online investing decisions. After you work through the review questions, the problem-solving exercises, and the fun and useful practice projects, you should be well on your way to achieving your goal of profitable online investing.

Q&A

1. Which of the following is a not-for-profit organization that maintains a Web site devoted to educating individual investors and helping them develop sound investment strategies?

   a. The New York Stock Exchange at www.nyse.org

   b. The Federal Trade Commission at www.ftc.gov

   c. The National Association of Independent Investors at www.better-investing.org

2. The investing principle that helps protect your portfolio against loss from adverse events that affect a particular company or industry is called _____.

3. *Dollar cost averaging* refers to which of the following practices?

   a. Investing regular amounts at regular time intervals

   b. Buying stocks costing an amount within an average range

   c. Buying stocks at a price consistent with their historical average cost

   d. Predicting future performance based on historical trends

4. An *index fund* is

   a. A mutual fund that discloses its performance publicly to the Morningstar mutual fund index

   b. A mutual fund that buys stocks that have a price point within an average indexed range

   c. A trust that funds research in the S&P Index

   d. A mutual fund that's designed to mirror the performance of a major stock index

5. Placing a stock trade after the NYSE or NASDAQ has closed for the day is made possible by using a(n)

_____.

6. A stock that's *not* listed on the New York Stock Exchange but that's traded on the NASDAQ is referred to as

a. A penny stock

b. An option

c. A high-risk investment

d. An over-the-counter stock

7. Datek Online offers a service that allows you to view continuous real-time quotes on your computer screen, which is called

_____.

8. A Web site that contains performance and customer satisfaction ratings of online brokers, as well as lists the services they provide, is

a. www.betterinvesting.com

b. www.edgar.gov

c. www.gobroke.com

d. www.gomez.com

9. The process of creating a list of stocks or mutual funds that meet your initial criteria and merit further research is called

_____.

10. Which of the following is a good source of accurate historical data reflecting a company's performance for the past five years?

a. Chat rooms

b. A company's annual report

c. A company's prospectus

d. www.morningstar.com

e. *Value Line Investment Survey*

11. The document that contains the income tax information reported to the IRS concerning your investment is _____.

12. At which of the following Web sites can you access all documents filed by a company with the Securities and Exchange Commission?

a. www.betterinvesting.com

b. www.sec.gov/edgarhp

c. www.gobroke.com

d. www.gomez.com

13. A *limit order* specifies a limit for _____
_____.

Answers: (1) c (2) diversification (3) a (4) d (5) Electronic Trading Network (6) d (7) streaming (8) d (9) screening (10) e (11) Form 1099 (12) b (13) the maximum or minimum price you're willing to pay

Scenarios

1. You have a stock mutual fund that experienced a loss in the last two months, but that is still profitable for the year. What do you do with the fund? _____
_____

2. Your investment portfolio consists of carefully selected small-cap, mid-cap and large-cap stocks diversified across industry sectors. What other investments should you consider adding to your portfolio? _____
_____

3. You own a stock that has always been profitable in the past, but has been lagging over the past nine months. You suspect it's because other competing companies have begun to market similar product lines. What do you do? _____
_____

4. A buddy from your Yahoo! Investment Club forwards a message about an imminent takeover of an obscure company, which is expected to send the price of the stock skyrocketing. The stock is only $3.50 a share. You're tempted. At $3.50 a share, how much can you lose?_____

_____

Answers: (1) The best course of action is to continue to watch the mutual fund, but probably not to sell your shares at this point. Investments fluctuate over the short term, and fees associated with mutual funds are a further deterrent to selling them to look for greener pastures over the short term. (2) You should invest 30 percent of your portfolio in bonds to achieve diversification and stability. (3) You should definitely research the events that may have adversely affected the company's market share and prepare a new Stock Selection Guide (SSG) form to further evaluate the situation. (4) You can lose $3.50 a share (your entire investment), plus brokerage commissions.

Consider This

- During no 20-year period in history has the stock market lost money. This includes the 20-year period spanning the Great Depression.

- Over the past 72 years, stock market growth has outpaced the rate of inflation by 3½ times. Stock market returns over the same period have been twice that of U.S. government bonds.

- The Dow Jones Industrial Average, the most widely reporting stock market tracking index, is based on the performance of just 30 stocks.

- The average actively managed mutual fund beat the performance of the average index fund in 1999 for the first time in ten years. In the past, index funds have outperformed actively managed mutual funds. Is this a fluke, or are fund managers becoming more skilled and savvy?

CLIFFSNOTES RESOURCE CENTER

The learning doesn't need to stop here. CliffsNotes Resource Center shows you the best of the best — links to the best information in print and online about online investing and the Internet. And don't think that this is all we've prepared for you; we've put all kinds of pertinent information at www.cliffsnotes.com. Look for all the terrific resources at your favorite bookstore or local library and on the Internet. When you're online, make your first stop www.cliffsnotes.com, where you'll find more incredibly useful information about online investing.

Books

This CliffsNotes book is just one of many great titles on investment and financial topics published by IDG Books Worldwide. If you want some great next-step books, check out these other publications.

CliffsNotes Investing in the Stock Market, by C. Edward Gilpatric, provides a nuts-and-bolts approach to investing in the stock market and selecting stocks to meet specific investment goals. IDG Books Worldwide, Inc. $8.99.

Teach Yourself Investing Online, by Thomas S. Gray and Claire Mencke, allows visual learners to pick up on the ins and outs of online investing in an easy-to-understand visual format. IDG Books Worldwide, Inc. $19.99.

CliffsNotes Balancing Your Checkbook With Quicken, by Jill Gilbert, helps you avail yourself of some of the same conveniences for your online bank accounts that you enjoy for your brokerage accounts. This book also tells you how to track expenses for budgeting and tax purposes. IDG Books Worldwide, Inc. $8.99.

Mutual Funds For Dummies, 2nd Edition, by Eric Tyson, tells you everything you need to know to understand the fees and benefits associated with mutual fund investing. IDG Books Worldwide, Inc. $19.99.

Internet

Check out these Web sites for more information about online investing and more:

Investorama, www.investorama.com, provides links to thousands of articles and a searchable database you can use to research articles on a specific company.

IRS Web site, www.irs.ustreas.gov, is a great site maintained by the U.S. Treasury Department that enables you to access tax forms, tax pamphlets, informative publications, and news releases that can help you plan for taxes and meet your obligations as your portfolio grows.

Armchair Millionaire, www.armchairmillionaire.com, as its name indicates, tells you how to become a millionaire. It covers all the basics, including a plan for getting out of debt. Its "five steps to financial freedom" are worth perusing.

Save Wealth Estate Planning, www.savewealth.com, provides a great overview of living trusts and other estate planning options.

Magazines and Newspapers

Depending on your schedule and the frequency of your appetite for investment news, you can choose from among the following daily, weekly, biweekly, or monthly publications:

Investor's Business Daily offers daily updates on stock market activity, both concise and detailed coverage of news events, and commentaries considered to be some of the best in the industry. (www.investors.com) $197.00/year.

The Wall Street Journal **is another daily publication that keeps you current on stock market and business news. One of the oldest and most respected publications in the industry.** (www.wsj.com) **$159/mo.**

Forbes is a biweekly magazine that helps you keep track of investment news, industry developments, stock and mutual fund performance, and related trends. (www.forbes.com) $4.95/issue.

Fortune is a weekly publication that offers general business news about the events of the past week, analysis, and in-depth commentary. (www.pathfinder.com) $4.95/issue.

Money, a monthly business magazine, covers a variety of topics, trends, and stories about investment and tax saving. (www.money.com) $3.95/issue.

Send Us Your Favorite Tips

In your quest for learning, have you ever experienced that sublime moment when you figure out a trick that saves time or trouble? Perhaps you realized you were taking ten steps to accomplish something that could have taken two. Or you found a little-known workaround that gets great results. If you've discovered a useful tip that helped you invest online more effectively and you'd like to share it, the CliffsNotes staff would love to hear from you. Go to our Web site at www.cliffsnotes.com and click the Talk to Us button. If we select your tip, we may publish it as part of CliffsNotes Daily, our exciting, free e-mail newsletter. To find out more or to subscribe to a newsletter, go to on the Web.

INDEX

A

accounts
  annual summary, 96
  balance tracking, 96
  interest on idle funds, 72
  minimum balance, 7, 71
  opening, 77, 78, 95
  statements, 96
after-hours trading, 88, 89
American Association of Individual
  Investors (AAII), 17, 18
annual reports, 21, 35, 36, 97

B

bills (fixed-income securities), 61, 64
Bloomberg Web site, 99, 104
bond funds, 47, 61
Bond Market Association, 62
BondAgent.com, 61
bonds
  call features, 60
  corporate, 56
  coupon rate, 58, 60
  described, 55–59
  fixed return, 47
  government, federal, 56, 63–66
  government, foreign, 56
  government, local, 56
  government, state, 56
  grades, 57, 58
  inflation issues, 58–60
  inflation-indexed notes, 64
  issuing bodies, 9, 56–58
  junk bonds, 57
  maturity date, 47, 60, 61
  online research, 62
  rating, 10, 23, 57, 58, 60
  risk, 47, 57, 58, 60
  secondary market, 58, 60
  selling, 94
  taxes, 61
  yield, 59
Bonds Online, 10, 58, 59
Bonds Online Web site, 10
brokers
  choosing, 67–73
  contracts, 95
  licensing, 5
  NASD resources, 106, 107

  rating services, 68, 73–77
  responsibilities, 4, 5, 68
  SIPC insured, 68
Bureau of the Public Debt Web site,
  23, 63

C

CNBC Web site, 22, 80–82
commissions, 7, 69–71
commodities, 12
compounding, 20
connection alternatives, 89, 90

D

Datek Online, 81, 86–88
Datek Online Web site, 9
day trading, 20
Discount Stockbrokers Ranked
  (report), 77
diversification
  bonds, 47
  by company size, 27
  defined, 8
  investment principle, 19, 20
  mutual funds, 43
  NAIC recommendations, 26
  by sector, 27
Dividend Reinvestment Plans (DRIPs),
  78, 79
dollar cost averaging, 18, 19
Dow Jones Industrial Average, 22,
  46, 112
DRIP Central, 78

E

e-zines, 34
Electronic Data Gathering and Retrieval
  Service (EDGAR), 37, 38
Electronic Trading Networks
  (ECNs), 88

F

Federal Trade Commission (FTC),
  107, 108
fees, 7, 45, 46, 69–71, 88
fixed-income securities, 61
Forbes Mutual Fund Information
  Center, 11
futures, 12